THE COLONIAL OVERLORDS

TimeFrame AD 1850-1900

THE UNITED STATES

GERMANY

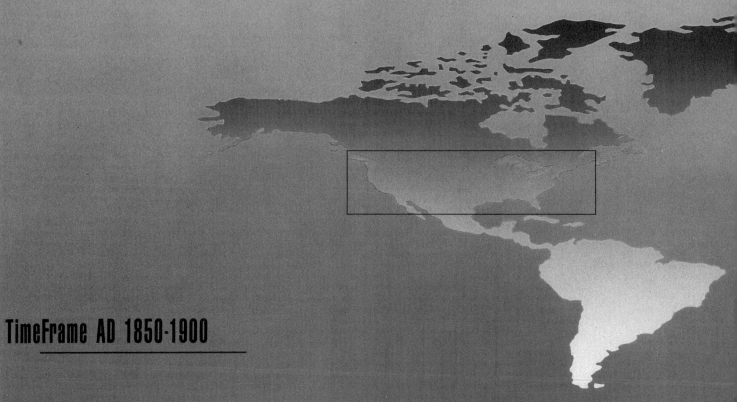

TimeFrame AD 1850-1900

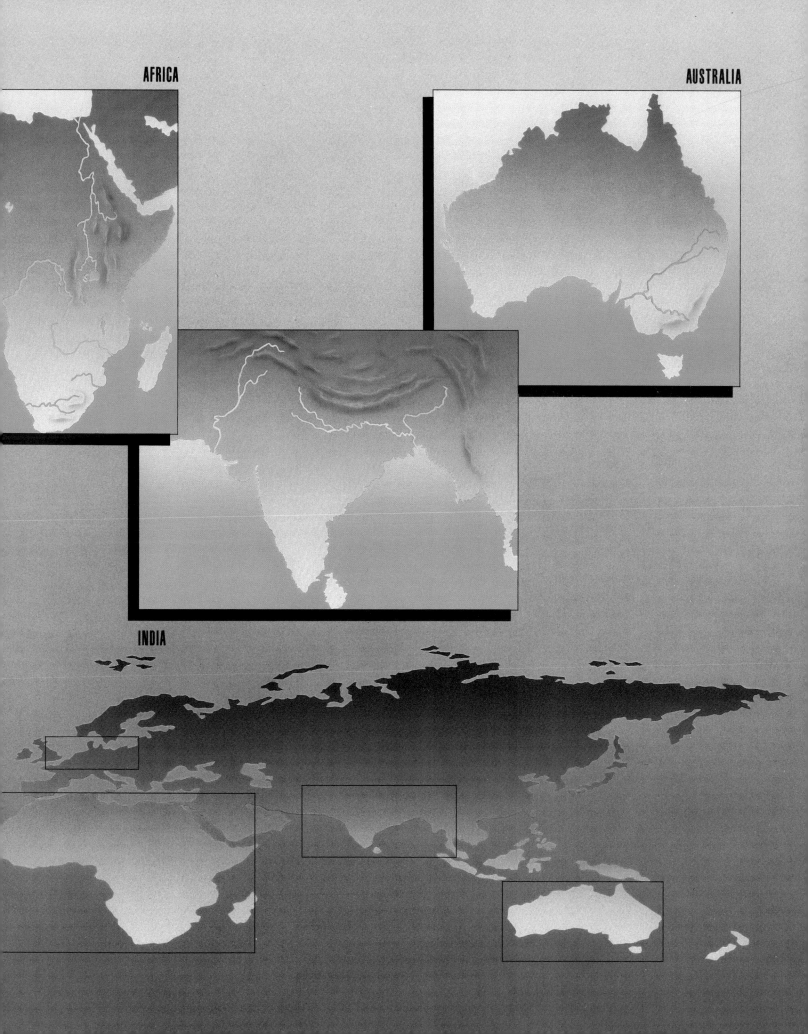

AFRICA

AUSTRALIA

INDIA

TIME® **LIFE** BOOKS

Other Publications:
AMERICAN COUNTRY
VOYAGE THROUGH THE UNIVERSE
THE THIRD REICH
THE TIME-LIFE GARDENER'S GUIDE
MYSTERIES OF THE UNKNOWN
FIX IT YOURSELF
FITNESS, HEALTH & NUTRITION
SUCCESSFUL PARENTING
HEALTHY HOME COOKING
UNDERSTANDING COMPUTERS
LIBRARY OF NATIONS
THE ENCHANTED WORLD
THE KODAK LIBRARY OF CREATIVE PHOTOGRAPHY
GREAT MEALS IN MINUTES
THE CIVIL WAR
PLANET EARTH
COLLECTOR'S LIBRARY OF THE CIVIL WAR
THE EPIC OF FLIGHT
THE GOOD COOK
WORLD WAR II
HOME REPAIR AND IMPROVEMENT
THE OLD WEST

For information on and a full description of
any of the Time-Life Books series listed above,
please call 1-800-621-7026 or write:
Reader Information
Time-Life Customer Service
P.O. Box C-32068
Richmond, Virginia 23261-2068

This volume is one in a series that tells the story
of humankind. Other books in the series include:
The Age of God-Kings
Barbarian Tides
A Soaring Spirit
Empires Ascendant
Empires Besieged
The March of Islam
Fury of the Northmen
Light in the East
The Divine Campaigns
The Mongol Conquests
The Age of Calamity
Voyages of Discovery
The European Emergence
Powers of the Crown
Winds of Revolution
The Pulse of Enterprise
The World in Arms
Shadow of the Dictators

THE COLONIAL OVERLORDS

TimeFrame AD 1850-1900

BY THE EDITORS OF TIME-LIFE BOOKS

TIME-LIFE BOOKS, ALEXANDRIA, VIRGINIA

Time-Life Books Inc.
is a wholly owned subsidiary of
THE TIME INC. BOOK COMPANY

President and Chief Executive Officer:
Kelso F. Sutton
President, Time Inc. Books Direct:
Christopher T. Linen

TIME-LIFE BOOKS INC.

EDITOR: George Constable
Director of Design: Louis Klein
Director of Editorial Resources:
Phyllis K. Wise
Director of Photography and Research:
John Conrad Weiser

EUROPEAN EDITOR: Ellen Phillips
Executive Editor: Gillian Moore
Design Director: Ed Skyner
Assistant Design Director: Mary Staples
Chief of Research: Vanessa Kramer
Chief Sub-Editor: Ilse Gray

PRESIDENT: John M. Fahey, Jr.
Senior Vice Presidents: Robert M.
DeSena, Paul R. Stewart, Curtis G.
Viebranz, Joseph J. Ward
Vice Presidents: Stephen L. Bair,
Bonita L. Boezeman, Mary P. Donohoe,
Stephen L. Goldstein, Juanita T. James,
Andrew P. Kaplan, Trevor Lunn, Susan J.
Maruyama, Robert H. Smith
New Product Development: Trevor Lunn,
Donia Ann Steele
Supervisor of Quality Control: James King

PUBLISHER: Joseph J. Ward

Correspondents: Elisabeth Kraemer-Singh
(Bonn); Christina Lieberman (New York);
Maria Vincenza Aloisi (Paris); Ann
Natanson (Rome). Valuable assistance
was also provided by: Angie Lemmer
(Bonn); John Dunn (Melbourne); Eliza-
beth Brown (New York); Ann Wise
(Rome).

TIME FRAME
(published in Britain as
TIME-LIFE HISTORY OF THE WORLD)

SERIES EDITOR: Tony Allan

Editorial Staff for *The Colonial
Overlords:*
Editor: Charles Boyle
Designer: Lynne Brown
Researcher: Caroline Lucas
Sub-Editor: Frances Willard
Design Assistant: Rachel Gibson
Editorial Assistant: Molly Sutherland
Picture Department: Amanda Hindley
(administrator), Jeroen Bergmans (picture
coordinator)

Editorial Production
Chief: Samantha Hill
Traffic Coordinator: Emma Veys
Editorial Department: Theresa John,
Debra Lelliott

U.S. EDITION

Assistant Editor: Barbara Fairchild
Quarmby
Copy Coordinator: Elizabeth Graham
Picture Coordinator: Barry Anthony

Editorial Operations
Production: Celia Beattie
Library: Louise D. Forstall

Computer Composition: Gordon E. Buck
(Manager), Deborah G. Tait, Monika D.
Thayer, Janet Barnes Syring, Lillian
Daniels

Special Contributors: Nicholas Best, John
Cottrell, Windsor Chorlton, Ellen Galford
(text); Neil Fairbairn, Sheila Corr
(research); David E. Manley (index).

CONSULTANTS

General:
GEOFFREY PARKER, Professor of History,
University of Illinois, Urbana-Champaign,
Illinois

General and India:
CHRISTOPHER BAYLY, Reader in Modern Indian History, Saint Catharine's College, Cambridge University, Cambridge,
England

Germany:
JONATHAN STEINBERG, Lecturer in His-
tory, Trinity Hall, Cambridge University,
Cambridge, England

Southern Africa:
RICHARD RATHBONE, Reader in the
Contemporary History of Africa, School of
Oriental and African Studies, University of
London, England

Australia:
CARL BRIDGE, Senior Lecturer in History,
University of New England, New South
Wales, Australia

The United States:
HUGH BROGAN, Senior Lecturer in History, University of Essex, Colchester, England

**Library of Congress Cataloging in
Publication Data**

The Colonial overlords: timeframe AD 1850-
1900 / by the editors of Time-Life Books.
    p.   cm. — (Time frame series)
    Includes bibliographical references (p.   )
and index.
    ISBN 0-8094-6466-7
    ISBN 0-8094-6467-5 (lib. bdg.)
    1. History, Modern—19th century.
I. Time-Life Books. II. Series. Time frame.
D358.C57 1990
909.81—dc20   90-11095
                                          CIP

Time-Life Books Inc. offers a wide range of fine
recordings, including a *Rock 'n' Roll Era* series.
For subscription information, call 1-800-621-
7026 or write Time-Life Music, P.O. Box C-
32068, Richmond, Virginia 23261-2068.

CONTENTS

1 **High Noon of the Raj** 8

Essay: A Blaze of Progress 35

2 **Germany's Iron Chancellor** 42

Essay: Feeding the Multitudes 65

3 **The Scramble for Africa** 74

Essay: The People's Art 103

4 **The Shaping of Australia** 110

5 **America Divided** 130

Essay: Undercurrents of Anxiety 163

Chronology 168
Acknowledgments 170
Picture Credits 170
Bibliography 171
Index 173

HIGH NOON OF THE RAJ

"The secret of the mastery of the world is, if they only knew it, in the possession of the British people." These words of Lord Curzon, written four years before he was appointed viceroy of India in 1898, were a clarion call to his compatriots to hold fast to the greatest empire on earth. He had no doubt that the destiny of all the world's underdeveloped regions had been entrusted by Providence to the British, and it was their bounden duty to diffuse the civilizing influence of British rule across the globe.

Curzon had traveled twice around the world, and his beliefs were founded upon first-hand experience of many different societies. He knew—and hence the note of frustration in his words—that he did not speak for all his countrymen, that there were many who were either indifferent toward the colonies or who regarded them as merely the means to further short-term commercial interests. But Curzon's conviction that the empire was a crusade dedicated to the improvement of mankind was sincere and immensely persuasive, and during the latter half of the nineteenth century, it inspired empire builders in many other countries besides Britain.

Each nation sent armies to further its goals. Campaigns were fought in the mountain passes of Afghanistan and the alluvial plains of China, the desert wastes of the Sudan and the swampy deltas of Southeast Asia. Preceding and following the armies surged explorers, merchants, missionaries, politicians, artists, philanthropists, engineers, teachers, and scientists. As a result of their collective endeavors, European nations had won control over four-fifths of the land surface of the globe by 1900. Britain was master of Canada, Australia, India, southern Arabia, and large parts of Africa; the French were established in West Africa and in Southeast Asia; Russian influence had steadily expanded across northern Asia; and latecomers such as Germany and Italy competed with earlier imperial powers such as Spain and Portugal for the parts of Africa not already claimed by the British and French. America too had not only extended its western frontier to the Pacific Ocean, but had seized overseas territories from the declining empire of Spain. Even in the remote islands of Polynesia in the South Pacific, the Scottish writer Robert Louis Stevenson felt the reverberations of "a stir-about of epochs and races, barbarisms and civilizations, virtues and crimes."

The motives that powered the massive expansion of European power were in fact far more complex than Curzon or any other single participant in the imperialist drive could comprehend. The sense of moral superiority felt by many Europeans derived in part from the great material advances following the Industrial Revolution, which had made Europe far richer than other parts of the world in money, technology, and expertise. Their economy rapidly expanding, Europeans needed foreign markets for their products, and they developed an appetite for exotic imports and agricultural products. Also, Europe was divided by nationalist rivalries, so that where one nation reached out, its competitor was determined to reach out farther. Germany in par-

A painting by an Indian artist shows a British child, accompanied by three servants, enjoying a horseback ride in a Calcutta garden in the 1840s. By then, the East India Company had brought almost all of India under British control, and Calcutta had become the administrative and intellectual capital of the subcontinent. Within ten years, the British government had taken over direct control, and an Indian population of some 250 million bowed to the imperial might of the British raj.

9

In the last quarter of the nineteenth century, the nations of Europe, whose possessions in Asia and Africa had so far consisted mostly of isolated trading settlements, extended their reach into the interiors of these continents and competed against one another for global dominance. The largest empires, as shown on the map, were the British *(shaded pink)* and French *(shaded pale green)*; Germany, Portugal, the United States, the Netherlands, Spain, Italy, and Belgium also ruled overseas territories. By 1900, scarcely a region of the world remained immune from European influence.

India—whose shape on the map resembled, in the eyes of one British administrator's daughter, an ice-cream cone—was the linchpin of the British empire, the territory that excited most pride in its conquerors. After the Indian Mutiny of 1857, military campaigns were fought only along the North-West Frontier and in Burma; the British maintained their control over the rest of the subcontinent by the diligence of around 1,000 highly trained civil servants and by the careful supervison of native Indian princes.

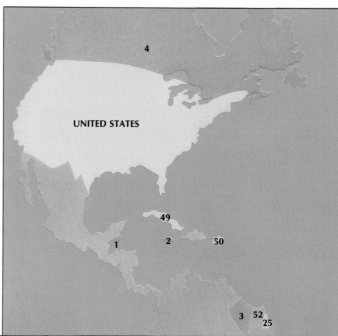

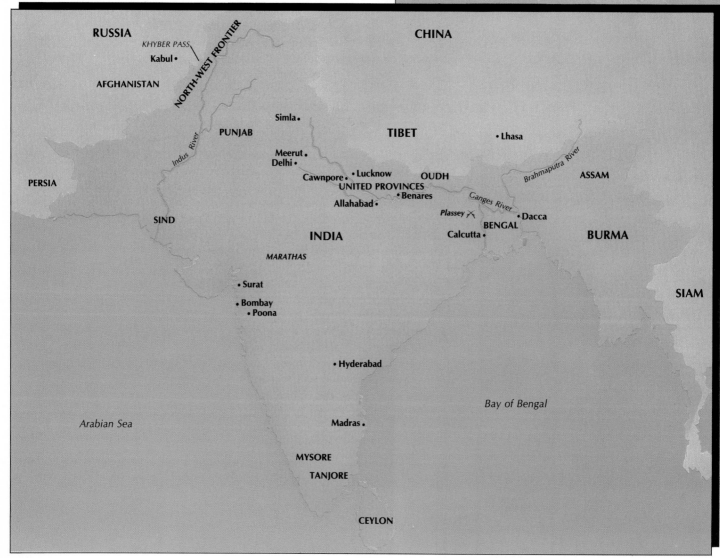

HOLLAND

BRITAIN
BELGIUM — GERMANY

FRANCE

PORTUGAL — SPAIN   ITALY

BRITAIN
1 British Honduras
2 Jamaica
3 British Guiana
4 Canada
5 Gambia
6 Sierra Leone
7 Gold Coast
8 Nigeria
9 Egypt
10 Sudan
11 British East Africa
12 Nyasaland
13 Rhodesia
14 Bechuanaland
15 South Africa
16 British Somaliland
17 Aden
18 India
19 Malaya
20 Sarawak
21 North Borneo
22 British New Guinea
23 Australia
24 New Zealand

FRANCE
25 French Guiana
26 Senegal
27 Algeria
28 Tunis
29 French Guinea
30 Mauritania
31 Ivory Coast
32 Dahomey
33 French Sudan
34 French Equatorial Africa
35 French Congo
36 French Somaliland
37 Madagascar
38 French Indochina

GERMANY
39 Togo
40 Cameroons
41 German Southwest Africa
42 German East Africa
43 German New Guinea

PORTUGAL
44 Portuguese Guinea

45 Cabinda
46 Angola
47 Mozambique
48 Portuguese Timor

UNITED STATES
49 Cuba
50 Puerto Rico
51 Philippine Islands

HOLLAND
52 Dutch Guiana
53 Dutch East Indies

SPAIN
54 Río de Oro
55 Río Muni

ITALY
56 Eritrea
57 Italian Somaliland

BELGIUM
58 Leopold's Congo

ticular, newly unified under Chancellor Otto von Bismarck, was determined to match Britain both in industrial might and overseas influence. All these factors combined to set in motion a process that, once started, became unstoppable. The appetite for empire would change the destinies of many millions of lives in the subject nations, and it would shape the course of the twentieth century.

The largest of the European empires was the British, and its most prized domain—compensating for Britain's loss of its American colonies in the eighteenth century—was India. It was as large as Europe itself, inhabited by one-quarter of the world's population; its languages and faiths were many and ancient, and it had long experience of foreign rule. Earlier conquerors had entered its fertile plains by crossing the high northwestern mountain ranges that divided India from central Asia. The British took a different route: They arrived as merchants, knocking at the back door.

When the East India Company was chartered by Elizabeth I in 1600, its primary commercial goal had been the spice harvests of the Malay Archipelago, and it was keenly aware of Spanish, Portuguese, and Dutch competition. Sir Thomas Roe, who in 1612 negotiated permission for the company to build its first trading post in India at the port of Surat, on the western coast, warned that it would be "an error to affect

At the head of this procession, depicted by an Indian artist around 1830, the rajah of Tanjore (modern-day Thanjavur), the ruler of a state in southeast India, rides in a howdah on a richly caparisoned elephant; following close behind on a bay horse is the British resident. The presence of a resident was one of the conditions imposed on many Indian states by the terms of treaties they signed with the East India Company. Although officially forbidden to interfere with internal affairs, residents kept a close watch over the Indian rulers and over British interests in their territories.

garrisons and land wars in India," and during its early years, the company concentrated on building up a network of peaceful trading posts. But as its holdings grew, so did its ambitions. In 1640, the company leased from a Hindu ruler land on which to build a fort; that center came to be called Madras, destined to become one of the three great port cities of Britain's Indian empire. In 1668, the company acquired Bombay, an island that had come to the Crown as part of the dowry of Charles II's Portuguese bride, and from this new base on the west coast, the company looked with longing at the eastern province of Bengal, with its abundant saltpeter and textiles.

The time was ripe, declared Sir Josiah Child, appointed chairman of the company in 1681, to lay "the foundation of a large, well-grounded, sure English dominion in India for all time to come." An expedition was sent to Bengal, and the Mogul emperor of India—distracted by wars against an emergent Hindu power, the Marathas—granted the company the rights of landlord in three villages 100 miles upriver from the Bay of Bengal. The site was a malarial swamp with a deep-water anchorage; few could have imagined it would be transformed into the third great entrepôt of colonial power, the populous, frenetic port of Calcutta—"the many-sided, the smoky, the magnificent City of Dreadful Night," as Rudyard Kipling was to call it.

By now, Britain's chief European commercial rivals in India were the French, and

in the mid-eighteenth century, wars between the two countries in Europe led to armed conflict in the subcontinent. The British emerged victorious, and with far richer spoils than they had envisaged—a former East India company clerk named Robert Clive, after driving the French out of Bengal, defeated the local Muslim ruler at the Battle of Plassey in 1757 and established the company as a major political power. After a period of financial chaos in which Clive and other officials plundered Bengal, exacting huge tributes and trading at great personal profit, the British government was compelled to take some responsibility for the company's possessions. By the Regulating Act of 1773, Warren Hastings—Clive's successor in the company hierarchy—was appointed governor general, Madras and Bombay were brought under the control of Bengal, and Hastings's council was augmented by four members appointed by Parliament. Eleven years later, a government under the leadership of Prime Minister William Pitt passed the India Act, which made the company directors subservient to a board of control—comprising between three and six cabinet ministers—that had complete authority over "the levying of war or making of peace, or negotiating with any of the native princes or states in India."

A mid-nineteenth-century watercolor shows three Indian bandits strangling their victim before robbing him. The perpetrators of this ritual crime, known as thuggee, were believed to be fanatical devotees of Kālī, the Hindu goddess of destruction; following the decline of the Mogul empire, they were joined by large numbers of common criminals. Beginning in the 1830s, the British, supported by law-abiding Indians, made determined efforts to eradicate this menace to travelers.

Lacking faith in company men, Pitt installed as governor general one of his own protégés, Lord Cornwallis, an army commander who went further than any of his predecessors in putting a British stamp on India. Seeking to root out corruption and dishonesty, he separated the company into commercial and political branches, and he raised the salaries of his administrators, thereby creating a loyal professional body—a prototype civil service—from which Indians were excluded. To finance these changes, he reformed Bengal's revenue and land system, and he imposed a company monopoly on the collection, sale, and importation of salt.

Despite Pitt's stated objection to territorial acquisitions, Cornwallis found himself drawn into a war in the south, where Madras was threatened by Tipu Sultan—the "Tiger of Mysore," or citoyen Tipu as he was later to be called from his connivance with Napoleon Bonaparte. Tipu was defeated in 1792 and forced to cede territory to the British. The process of British expansion—in the interests of making their frontiers secure, and of unifying their holdings so as to reap the full benefits of trade and commerce—was now in train, and was aided by divisions in Indian society. The power of the Mogul empire, which had dominated northern India for nearly three centuries, was rapidly waning, and rivalries between individual Indian rulers prevented their coming together to resist the British.

In 1797, Lord Mornington, later Marquis Wellesley, was appointed governor general with instructions to root out all remaining pockets of French influence. Aided by his brother Arthur, the future duke of Wellington, Wellesley mounted a vigorous campaign that ended with the annexation of almost half of Mysore. Wellesley then seized half the northern state of Oudh (present-day Uttar Pradesh) and imposed treaties on other Indian states by which the company guaranteed their independence in return for control of their foreign relations. In further campaigns against the Marathas, a confederacy of Hindu rulers in western India, the British secured the city of Delhi, and the Mogul emperor was reduced to the status of a company pensioner. The Marathas were not entirely crushed until 1818, but by the time Wellesley was recalled in 1805, British domination of India was beyond dispute.

"When I recollect," worried the president of the Board of Control in 1804, "that the number of Europeans civil and military governing 50 millions of subjects, do not

Hindu temples dominate the crowded banks of the Ganges in the holy city of Benares (present-day Varanasi) in northeast India. The British ignorance of Hinduism and the several other faiths of the subcontinent, coupled with the activities of Christian missionaries, contributed to the resentment of their rule that fueled the Indian Mutiny of 1857. The British later pursued a policy of noninterference, in line with the advice given by Sir Bartle Frere to the first viceroy: "Let not government presume to dictate to the meanest of its subjects what he shall believe."

exceed 30,000, I cannot but look with anxiety to the extension of our native population and dependencies.'' But the British could hardly pack up their bags and leave: Having acquired so much territory and developed such profitable trading links, they were now committed to rule in India. Establishing military control was the most urgent task, since central India was being ravaged by disbanded soldiers and gangs of robbers. By 1824, the company's armies contained no fewer than 170 regiments of Indian soldiers, known as sepoys, in addition to 16 European regiments—about 200,000 men in all, making it the largest modern army in Asia. Commerce was another priority, and the company's trade monopolies—except of opium (British India's major export to China) and salt—were abolished. Free trade proved one-sided, however; Bengal was soon flooded with cheap English cotton, bringing about the collapse of the province's vast textile industry and throwing millions out of work.

Hand in hand with the new commercial spirit went that of Christian evangelism. The latter's most eloquent advocate, William Wilberforce, declared that the British could best carry out their responsibilities to their Indian subjects ''by the gradual introduction and establishment of our own principles and opinions; of our laws, institutions, and manners; above all, as the source of every other improvement, of our religion, and consequently of our morals." These suggestions were acted upon by Lord William Bentinck, governor general from 1828 to 1835, who abolished the Hindu practice of sati—the burning of widows on the funeral pyres of their husbands—and took stern action against thuggee, the ritual murder of travelers by Hindu robbers who had supposedly pledged themselves to the service of the goddess Kālī. Even more significantly, Bentinck established schools and colleges charged with imparting knowledge of Western culture and science in the English language.

In his campaign against sati, Bentinck was supported by a Bengali former company servant named Ram Mohun Roy, who founded a Hindu reform movement to meet the British challenge to his religion. Roy established secondary schools and the first Indian-run newspapers, which he and his successors used to advance their own ideas of how India could be reformed to meet the needs of the new age. Few other Indians had access to the corridors of power. In theory, high company posts were now open to Indians, but since 1806, admission was dependent on passing examinations at the company's college in England. Since Hindus were forbidden for religious reasons to travel overseas, the administration remained the preserve of British recruits—young, ignorant of India, and convinced of their innate superiority.

Moreover, the lifestyle of these new arrivals was very different from that of previous generations. In the eighteenth century, company servants had enjoyed frequent contact with the local rulers, and on the whole, they had treated one another as social equals. Far from trying to impose their own culture, the East India employees found themselves adopting Indian tastes and habits: Many had Indian friends, wore a version of Indian dress, smoked hookahs, and delighted in the sensual pleasures of dancing girls or amusements such as cockfighting or elephant-fighting. The scholars among them discussed Persian literature with Muslim nobles or debated philosophy with Hindu pundits. Cut off from England by a six-month sea voyage, some took Indian wives and many more kept Indian mistresses. Now, however, many recruits brought their wives, known in India as memsahibs (from the combination of the English *ma'am* and the Indian *sahib,* a term of respect for men of high social status), who were determined to keep their menfolk healthy in mind and body. In 1840, company servants were officially forbidden to participate in Indian religious festivals. The British kept themselves apart from their Indian subjects, and in the distance between the two communities, prejudice, ignorance, and suspicion flourished.

At the same time, the British were acquiring more territory and more subjects. Between 1824 and 1826, a war with Burma secured the northeastern border region and yielded Assam. Perceiving a threat from Russia, the "prowling bear," the British mounted a disastrous campaign to occupy Afghanistan, from which a lone survivor rode back through the Khyber Pass to tell of the destruction of an army 16,000 strong. As compensation for this blow to their prestige, the British conquered the northwestern provinces of Sind and Punjab.

To tidy up the internal map and secure more revenue, Lord Dalhousie annexed many territories that were still nominally independent. Under the spurious doctrine of "lapse," an Indian prince could be disinherited if he had no legitimate son or if the British judged him to be debauched or depraved. The annexation of Oudh in 1856, despite a long-standing alliance, was particularly inflammatory.

One reason for these aggressive territorial policies was to impress the Indians with a show of force. In a confidential report written after the Afghanistan fiasco of 1842, Charles Trevelyan, a senior company official, said: "We are, I fear, notwithstanding

Shreds of clothing and broken pots litter the Bibighar, the building in Cawnpore (Kanpur) in which 200 British women and children were massacred by Indian mutineers in June 1857. The victims were thrown down a well; the floor of the Bibighar, according to General James Neill, who took command of Cawnpore in July, remained "saturated with blood." This atrocity inflamed the British, who in the final stages of the mutiny wreaked vengeance on the rebels with equal ferocity.

all our efforts for the good of the people, an unpopular domination. We cannot afford to lose a battle. The first defeat would be the signal for a general uprising.'' He continued: ''The political feeling against us in India as foreigners and destroyers of the independence of so many races and states is very strong. . . . The religious feeling against us, and particularly the religious feeling of the Muhammadans, is a still more dangerous element.''

But these warnings were not heeded by Lord Canning, who in 1856, his first year as governor general, passed a law that obliged any future recruit to the Bengal army to serve overseas if so commanded—an order that conflicted with Hindu restrictions on foreign travel. Discontent among the Hindus grew when Canning passed another act permitting Hindu widows to remarry, against all the traditions of their faith. Taken together with the strident missionary work and Dalhousie's annexation of independent princedoms, it looked like a concerted effort to force a Christian moral code on India.

Rumors spread. The sepoys were to be blown up by mines as they assembled on parade grounds; Indian landlords were to be compelled to marry Crimean war widows so that their estates would eventually pass into Christian hands; the flesh of pigs and cows had been thrown into wells to pollute the water. For Muslims, the pig was ritually unclean; for Hindus, the cow was sacred. At the beginning of 1857, an Indian worker engaged in the preparation of new Enfield rifles shortly to be issued allegedly told a Hindu sepoy that the cartridges were greased with cow and pig fat. The story, which was untrue, spread like wildfire, and in early February, the first mutterings of a possible mutiny reached British ears.

The aged Bahādur Shāh II, the last of the Mogul dynasty of emperors who had ruled India since the sixteenth century, reclines on a couch with a hookah, an Oriental water-cooled pipe. A scholarly recluse, fond of music, poetry, and calligraphy, he was persuaded to lend his authority to the anti-British uprising in 1857. After the mutiny had been quelled he was exiled to Burma, where he died in 1862.

On Saturday, May 9, 1857, some 2,000 European troops and a slightly larger number of sepoys stood at attention on the parade ground at Meerut, a large British military base about forty-five miles northeast of Delhi. They watched impassively as eighty-five Indian troopers of the mainly Muslim 3d Light Cavalry were stripped of their uniforms and fettered in irons. Seventeen days earlier, they had refused to load their rifles with the new cartridges that had been issued. A court-martial had been convened and all the men found guilty of mutiny. Recommendations for clemency had been refused, and the mutineers were sentenced to ten years' imprisonment.

It took more than an hour to shackle them. Some accepted their humiliation with resignation. Others begged the commanding officer, Major General W. H. Hewitt, for mercy; when their appeal went unanswered they abused their comrades for not helping them. As they were marched off barefoot, some threw their boots at the colonel who had ordered the cartridges. ''There was a good deal of murmuring in our ranks,'' recorded Hugh Gough, a young British officer, ''and had it not been for the presence of British troops, it is impossible to say what might have taken place.''

Attended by Abdul Karim, one of two Indian servants whom she employed as secretaries from 1887 until her death in 1901, Queen Victoria writes at her desk in Balmoral Castle in Scotland. Victoria was the first British sovereign to take a personal interest in the empire, although she never visited India, and it was following her own suggestion that she was proclaimed empress of India in 1876.

Later that day, an Indian officer secretly warned Gough that the troops intended to release their comrades, but when Gough informed his colonel, he was rebuked for "listening to such idle tales." The next day, the Europeans in Meerut commented on the absence of domestic servants in their cantonment and speculated about the placards that had been seen in the city calling on Muslims to rise and slaughter the English. But the morning and afternoon passed without incident, and preparations for the evening church parade went ahead as usual. Gough was dressing for the parade when a servant dashed in to tell him that the sepoy quarters were ablaze.

All three sepoy regiments at Meerut had risen in revolt. At about 5:00 p.m., men of the 3d Light Cavalry had stormed the barracks jail and released their imprisoned comrades. Shouting that the British were coming to disarm them, other sepoys had ransacked their weapons store and shot dead a British colonel. When Gough reached the sepoy quarters, he was met by "a maddened crowd of fiends and devils, all thirsting for the blood of their officers, and of Europeans generally."

The maharajah of Udaipur

The maharajah of Bundi

The maharajah of Jammu and Kashmir

The eldest son of the gaekwar of Baroda

A PRIDE OF PRINCES

"Providence," wrote the British poet and novelist Rudyard Kipling, "created the maharajahs to offer mankind a spectacle." But as the guardians of the age-old traditions of Indian rule, they had a political importance as well, and after the 1857 mutiny, the British government allowed the nearly 600 native princes to retain their authority over approximately one-quarter of the population of India.

While some of the princes remained bound by the customs of their forebears, others gradually adapted to Western ways. The nizam of Hyderabad, ruler of the largest and richest of the princely states, wore tailored woolen suits, entertained foreign royalty on tiger shoots, and appointed an official court photographer. Some of the sons and grandsons of the Indian princes chose to take up residence in London, where their extravagant lifestyles became a subject of fascination for the city's newspaper gossip columns.

The nizam of Hyderabad displays the tigers he has shot.

Indian and European high society are entertained at a banquet in the nizam's palace.

Joined by crowds of Indian civilians from the city, the mutineers made their way to the European quarters. Some sepoys and domestic servants risked their own lives trying to save officers and their families; but the mob was in a frenzy of passion, burning and plundering the bungalows, murdering Europeans and Indians alike, without distinction of age or sex. In an incident that was used to justify the atrocities later perpetrated by the British, the heavily pregnant wife of a British officer was killed by a Muslim butcher. Before the night ended, about fifty Europeans had been killed.

By then most of the mutineers, expecting a British counterattack, had fled Meerut and were heading for Delhi, the former capital of the Mogul empire. In the early morning of May 11, the leading horsemen reined in below the walls of the Red Fort on the eastern edge of the city and began clamoring for an audience with the titular emperor, Bahādur Shāh, last of the Mogul monarchs. Bahādur Shāh was in his eighties and a pensioner of the British, who were so sure of his submissiveness that they had not bothered to garrison Delhi with European troops, even though a huge magazine was located within the city. On Bahādur Shāh's instructions, the commander of his guard ordered the mutineers to disperse, but Muslim soldiers opened the city gates. A rabble swarmed toward the Red Fort, murdering any Europeans they met. Entering the royal precincts, where they killed the guard commander and several other British men and women, they finally confronted the terrified emperor. Pros-

An Indian woodcut *(right)* from around 1870 shows a train with separate carriages for Europeans and for Indian men and women. The opulent grandeur of the Victoria Terminus in Bombay *(above right)* advertises the scale and importance of the rail network that the British constructed throughout the subcontinent, enabling a journey from the north to the south of India to be completed in days rather than weeks.

trating themselves, the mutineers begged Bahādur Shāh to assume command in a war against English rule. He prevaricated, expecting the revolt to be crushed within hours.

Incredibly, the British troops had not been ordered to pursue the rebels; the obese and elderly General Hewitt was concerned only about the possibility of further trouble at Meerut. During the afternoon, the survivors there heard a rumbling explosion as the magazine at Delhi was blown up by British officers. This desperate act and the onset of evening convinced the sepoy regiments based outside Delhi that no British attack was forthcoming. They went over to the rebels, putting greater pressure on Bahādur Shāh who, frightened and confused, finally gave in. At midnight, a twenty-one-gun salute proclaimed that Bahādur Shāh had been restored to imperial glory.

To the Muslim faithful, it seemed that a prophecy had been fulfilled. For 100 years, it was said, a foreign power would rule over India; 1857, they reminded one another, was the centennial of the Battle of Plassey, which had made the British masters of Bengal. To some of the British, too, the fall of Delhi and the rapid spread of the rebellion seemed to spell the imminent collapse of their rule. In all of India there were

only 37,000 British troops, as against more than 230,000 Indian soldiers. In Calcutta, the seat of government in Bengal, British civilians took refuge on ships to escape the anticipated attack. At Simla, the British summer capital in the foothills of the Himalayas, the European residents fled after a rumor that a nearby Gurkha battalion had mutinied.

The Indian Mutiny, however, did not become a revolution. Most of the rebels' supporters were peasants and landlords whose lives had been disrupted by land reforms earlier in the century; overassessment of taxes and the introduction of deeds of tenure, many of which were taken over by bankers and moneylenders who had no compunction about evicting tenants, had caused widespread discontent, which was now catalyzed into violence by the shock waves of the mutiny. But these irregular forces lacked discipline, strong leadership, and a coherent strategy, and support from other sectors of Indian society was not forthcoming. The Sikhs of recently annexed Punjab hated the Hindus and welcomed the chance to settle old scores by fighting on the side of the British. Most of the semi-independent princes and the English-educated middle classes supported the British, for reasons of self-interest. In general, the rebellion was confined to north and central India along the Ganges, and its violence was most severe in Cawnpore (present-day Kanpur), Lucknow, and Delhi.

At Cawnpore in early June, the British commander faced the hopeless task of protecting some 900 men, women, and children in a makeshift camp on open ground close to the Ganges. For eighteen days he held out, losing all sixty of his gunners to murderous fire and many more defenders to sunstroke as temperatures climbed higher than 135° F. On June 23, the defenders repulsed an assault and were offered safe passage to Allahabad in return for their surrender. But no sooner had they climbed into the waiting boats than gunfire poured into them. Almost every man was killed, and the surviving women and children, some 200 in all, were taken back into the city and confined in a two-room building known as the Bibighar, or "House of the Ladies." Fearing the imminent arrival of a British relief force, the Indian leader ordered his troops to shoot these prisoners; when the soldiers refused, ruffians were sent in with swords and knives. Just one day after this massacre, the relief army arrived; a British official reported that inside the Bibighar, "the plaster was scored with sword cuts: not high up, as where men have fought, but low down, and about the corners, as if a creature had crouched to avoid a blow."

At the end of June, the mutiny reached Lucknow, where almost 3,000 people, nearly half of them Indians, were entrenched within the compound of the British chief commissioner's residency. A sortie against the mutineers on June 30 resulted in heavy casualties and the loss of five guns. Two days later, the chief commissioner was mortally wounded by a shell that burst in his room. The attackers kept the defenders under constant sniper fire and shelled the buildings to rubble, while sappers undermined the defenses and tried to blow up the walls. Inside, the defenders suffered dreadfully from sickness, vermin, and the stench of carrion. Many Indian sepoys deserted, and in the rat-infested cellars, the women debated whether they should commit suicide rather than risk falling into their attackers' hands.

In an 1888 watercolor sketch, a district officer of the Indian Civil Service presides over a court of law in the northwestern province of Punjab. His clerks sit cross-legged on the floor behind him, while plaintiffs and witnesses stand behind a rail. A British official still in his twenties might be responsible for the administration of a territory of more than one million inhabitants, and the cases brought before him could range from murders to appeals against tax assessments and accusations of witchcraft. Steering a tactful course between British legal principles and local traditions of Hindu or Muslim customary law, the district officers eventually made all of British India subject to an impartial code of justice.

On September 25, a relief column of kilted Highlanders burst into the compound, but they were unable to evacuate the garrison. And so the blockade dragged on until the end of October, when word reached Lucknow that a second relief force was on its way under the command of General Colin Campbell. A civilian clerk named Kavanagh volunteered to go through the enemy lines and guide the relieving force through the city and into the residency. Eight days later, he returned with Campbell's 4,000-strong force. After nearly five months, the siege of Lucknow was over. The number of Indians who were killed in the relief operation was uncountable; in one stronghold alone, nearly 2,000 sepoys were killed. No prisoners were taken.

Delhi, meanwhile, had fallen to the British. The mutineers' initial fervor had been dissipated by monsoon heat and squabbling among the emperor's advisers. While Bahādur Shāh sat in his rooms writing poetry, a British relief army swiftly approached the city. On September 14, the attack was launched, at the cost of nearly 1,200 British casualties. After a week of bloody street-fighting, most of the mutineers and the inhabitants of Delhi fled. Among them was Bahādur Shāh, but instead of escaping,

Victims of a famine that struck Madras and western India between 1876 and 1878, claiming several million lives, are shown in a photograph taken to raise funds for their relief. The British built networks of irrigation canals to combat the effects of floods, cyclones, and the failure of the monsoon rains—all common scourges of the subcontinent. A series of famine codes facilitated the building of relief centers, the transport of grain by rail to affected areas, and the development of projects to provide work and wages for the able-bodied.

he retreated to a tomb five miles from Delhi. William Hodson, leader of an irregular Sikh cavalry regiment, after promising Bahādur Shāh his life, escorted him back to Delhi. The next day, Hodson returned for two of Bahādur Shāh's sons and a grandson. No promises of safekeeping were given, and on the city's outskirts, he shot all three.

His action, which was generally admired by his colleagues, was mild compared to the bloody vengeance exacted elsewhere. In Delhi itself, one eyewitness boasted that "all the people found within the walls when our troops entered were bayoneted on the spot. . . . These were not mutineers but residents of the city, who trusted to our well-known mild rule for pardon. I am glad to say they were disappointed." At the site of the massacre of women in Cawnpore, the British made their captives lick the dried blood off the floor before hanging them. The war rumbled on until late in 1858, but the executions continued until well into 1859, rebels being hanged or shot without trial, convicted mutineers being lashed to the muzzles of guns and blown to pieces. Lord Canning tried in vain to curb the "rabid and indiscriminate vindictive-

An assortment of European-style buildings characterizes the main street of Simla, 7,000 feet high in the foothills of the Himalayas. During the hot summer months between April and mid-October, the government of India—in the persons of the viceroy and his senior officials—was transferred to this cool hill town, where gossip and intrigue were fanned by a continuous round of dances and parties.

ness" of his compatriots, pointing out that "the government which has punished blindly and revengefully will have lost its chief title to the respect of its subjects."

A death sentence was passed on the East India Company, too. Blamed by Parliament for having failed to gauge Indian public opinion, it was scrapped by the Government of India Act of 1858. All of the company's rights were transferred to the Crown, and full power for the government of India was vested in a secretary of state, who was assisted by a fifteen-member council. The governor general, elevated to the rank of viceroy, became the monarch's personal representative, gaining in prestige but not in power. The era of the British raj—from a Hindi word for rule—had begun.

The transfer of power was relatively straightforward; the company had long ceased to be a purely commercial organization, and most of the British in India already regarded themselves as the queen's as much as the company's servants. But for reasons of security, the army was completely reorganized. British soldiers in the company's armies were either paid off or absorbed into the British army. The Indian artillery was abolished, and the ratio of British to Indian troops was greatly increased.

The first new policy introduced after the war abolished the doctrine of lapse and recognized India's princes—the "breakwaters in the storm," as Canning called them—as an integral and important part of the imperial order. Intended to reward the princes for their loyalty during the mutiny, this policy also indicated a shift in Britain's whole approach. By allowing around one-quarter of the population of India to remain under the arbitrary rule of more than 560 princes, it ensured cultural continuity at the expense of national unity. The British had decided to play safe and abandoned their attempts to alter the traditional religious and cultural customs of their subjects. Officials were forbidden to interfere with native beliefs; missionaries were instructed to cut back on their proselytizing and direct their efforts into education. Economic and material projects were to be pursued and the social system left alone.

Of the public works undertaken, most attention was given to the development of the railway system, begun in the early 1850s. At the end of that decade, about 435 miles of track had been laid; by the end of the century, some 25,000 miles crisscrossed India. Side by side with the railways marched the telegraph, covering more

A British family gathers with their domestic staff on the lawn in front of their bungalow. A handbook published in 1878 recommended twenty-seven servants for a well-to-do family in Calcutta and fourteen for a bachelor. But despite this profusion of cooks and butlers, gardeners and nannies, the lot of British women in India—whose husbands were frequently absent on tours of duty, and whose children were sent to boarding school in England—was often loneliness and boredom.

than 18,600 miles by 1880. By the same date, almost 7.5 million acres of land in the United Provinces, Sind, and Punjab had been improved by irrigation projects.

In the beginning, the railroad benefited the British economy far more than the Indian. Since the subcontinent was rich in iron ore and coal, railway construction and operation could have provided the base for India's industrial development, but the track and rolling stock were manufactured in Britain; and after the opening of the Suez Canal in 1869, which reduced travel time between Britain and India from three months to three weeks, even the coal used to fire the locomotives was imported. Also, by bringing into the countryside cheap manufactured goods from Britain, the railways contributed to the decline of local handicraft industries.

The railroads, irrigation works, and other projects were coordinated by the Indian

Civil Service, known as the ICS, which numbered only 1,000 or so diligent and resourceful British men. These elite officials, called the "heaven-born" by admirers and "little tin gods" by their detractors, oversaw national and provincial affairs and administered the several hundred districts into which India was divided. After a brief apprenticeship with an experienced district officer, a young man in his twenties might find himself in charge of more than one million people, combining the roles of tax collector, policeman, and judge. But these roles by no means exhausted his duties. He might be called upon to hunt down a rogue tiger, settle land disputes, organize famine relief, inspect slaughterhouses, and award school prizes. He was essentially a talented amateur, selected less for his intellectual abilities than for leadership and authority, qualities inculcated by the English boarding schools at which most of the officials were educated. A district officer also had to possess an inexhaustible capacity for work: His contract specified that he be available for duty twenty-four hours a day, and often he was. "We were in the saddle by five in the morning," recalled one official, "and worked on horseback for two or three hours, riding about inspecting police stations, roads and bridges and public buildings under construction, tree-planting, ferry boats, settling disputes about land and property between villagers, and suchlike business." From ten in the morning until early evening, this officer worked as judge in the district court, where he relied less on a written code of laws than on his own experience and tact. "Our instructions were to decide all cases by the light of common sense and our own sense of what was just and right."

Closely involved with the day-to-day life of the country, most of the ICS officers learned to appreciate and admire the values of their Indian subjects and won their respect and trust. Just one year after the mutiny, when anti-Indian feeling was still widespread among the British, one officer wrote that "in spite of all that has happened, I take immense interest in the natives of India and like to be constantly among them." The hard work the officers put in was not for personal gain but for the benefit of the country they perceived it their duty to improve. "You ask why I am always thinking and talking of irrigation," wrote Sir Bartle Frere to a correspondent. "If you had seen men's bones, as I have, lying unburied by the roadside, and on entering a village had found it untenanted by a living person, you would understand why."

At the same time, however, in their social life the British resolutely abided by the same conventions as middle-class society in Victorian England, making no concessions to their very different environment. In lonely jungle stations, they still dressed for dinner, while their wives sweltered in heavy dresses shipped out from England. Most were married, for, after the opening of the Suez Canal, there was no shortage of English women in India; each year saw the arrival of a "fishing fleet" of prospective wives eager to snap up a "300-a-year dead-or-alive man"—a reference to the ICS starting salary and pension. To house the officials, new suburbs were built separate from the Indian towns, with bungalows on wide streets laid out for ease of troop movement; these cantonments contained their own stores as well as churches and the barracks of the British troops, and fraternizing with the nearby Indian community was officially frowned upon. Leaves were likely to be spent in England.

A rigid code of etiquette governed relations between the various ranks of the ICS,

A British cavalry officer of the Indian army *(left)* and an Indian infantryman *(right)* parade in their regimental uniforms. The British military force in India comprised regiments both of the regular British army and of the locally recruited Indian army. All senior officers in the latter were British, although a loyal Indian could rise to become a viceroy's commissioned officer, in charge of a company. After the mutiny, there were about 135,000 Indian troops and 62,000 British, and the proportion was maintained at roughly two to one.

and between the British and non-Europeans who aspired to British society. Among the latter were Anglo-Indians of mixed descent who were usually Christians and who referred to Britain as "home," although very few ever saw it, and English-speaking Indians who obtained menial posts in the administration. In fact, no class of Indians was treated with greater contempt than the clerks and pen-pushing functionaries known as babus, an honorific term that came to imply contempt for those whose education, patent-leather shoes, and genuine admiration for the British way of doing things merely confirmed their awkward status betwen one culture and another.

Despite an official declaration in 1853 that the competitive examinations for the ICS were open to all boys born in India, the fact that they were held in London—and the reduction of the age limit for taking them from twenty-three to nineteen—still effectively excluded Indians from the service. By 1869, only one Indian candidate, Surendranath Banerjea, had passed the examinations—and he was promptly disqualified on the grounds that his age as stated did not tally with the age he had given for a school examination four years earlier. After winning an appeal against the decision, he served in the ICS for three years before being dismissed for a minor infraction of rules. Unable to join the legal profession because of the discharge, he returned to Calcutta, where he worked as a teacher and journalist, and—in 1876—founded Bengal's first nationalist political organization, the Indian Association.

Among the issues on which Banerjea's association focused criticism were the civil-service-examination age limit, legislation against the Indian press, and the British free-trade policies that gave Lancashire cotton goods an advantage over Indian. But it was not a national organization; and Banerjea knew that, if nationalist demands were to be taken seriously by the British, it would be necessary to establish a forum in which voices from all over India could unite in protest.

The British themselves had already removed one obvious difficulty in the way of Indian unity: By teaching English in the schools established to train lawyers, teachers, and junior officials, they had helped to break down the language barriers that had previously divided the different regions of India. And it was the British who demonstrated to the Indian nationalists what could be achieved by united action.

In 1883, the viceroy, Lord Ripon, attempted to introduce legislation that would remove restrictions barring Indians in the British judicial service from trying criminal cases against Europeans. A year previously, the reform-minded Lord Ripon had sought to create municipal and district government boards filled largely by educated Indian officials and merchants—a human resource that, he considered, "it is not only bad policy, but sheer waste of power, to fail to utilize." That reform had been greeted with sullen dislike by the ICS; the new measure, however, raised a storm of wrath from all sections of the British community in India.

Denunciation of the proposed reform was violent and blatantly racist. "Would you like to live in a country," demanded the editor of one English newspaper, "where at any moment your wife would be liable to be sentenced on a false charge of slapping an ayah (Indian nurse or maidservant) to three days imprisonment, the magistrate being a copper-colored pagan who probably worships the linga, and certainly exults in any opportunity of showing that he can insult white persons with impunity?" The answer was a hysterical "No." Ripon was booed in the streets of Calcutta; hotheads conspired to kidnap him and send him back to Britain; the civil service publicly declared its opposition. Ripon caved in, producing a compromise that virtually ensured that Indians would play no part in the prosecution of British malefactors.

For Bengal's intelligentsia the outcome was a political eyeopener. If 100,000 Europeans could defeat the government of India by public protest, then how much more could a determined nation of some 250 million achieve? Two years later, seventy-three delegates from all over India met in Bombay and formally assumed the title of the Indian National Congress. Most were Hindu or Parsee lawyers, teachers, and journalists. Only two Muslims were present, and the nobility was unrepresented. Prominent among the organization's sponsors was a former East India Company servant, Allan Octavian Hume, a gentleman who twenty-five years earlier had incurred the scorn of his compatriots for his "excess of leniency" toward mutineers.

Other Britons supported the Congress's initially modest aspirations, which basically amounted to a claim for more extensive employment in the public service. But the administration was committed to retaining the old princely order and therefore saw the Congress, which represented the new educated professional class, as unrepresentative. It was an attitude shared by many non-Hindus, notably by Sir Sayyid Ahmad Khan, an anglophile intellectual who founded the Muslim Anglo-Oriental College in an attempt to bring his coreligionists into the sphere of political and economic power. "India is inhabited by different nationalities," he insisted. The activities of the Indian National Congress he saw as "fraught with dangers and suffering for all the nationalities of India, especially for the Muslims.'' The separatist sentiment nurtured by his college was to lead to the foundation of the Muslim League in 1906, and it was ultimately to contribute to partition between India and Pakistan.

Within the Congress itself, divergences over strategy and goals soon appeared. The opposing tendencies were personified by Gopāl Krishna Gokhale, leader of the moderate wing, and Bal Gangadhar Tilak, regarded as an extremist. Although an Indian patriot, Gokhale was also an admirer of Western culture who believed the British were a beneficial reforming force that would help India to take its place among the advanced nations of the world. By contrast, Tilak was a grass-roots nationalist who hoped to exploit the mass appeal of orthodox Hinduism to re-create the era of

The fortress of Bala Hissar (above) at Kabul in Afghanistan was stormed by British troops during the Afghan War of 1878 to 1880. Frequent campaigns were fought along the North-West Frontier, where the British sought control over Afghanistan to counter Russian expansion—a competition between the imperial powers that became known as the Great Game. Continually frustrated by the fierce resistance of Afghan tribes, notably the Afridis (right), the British signed a frontier agreement in 1887 and thereafter refrained from further interference in Afghan affairs.

Maratha glory. In 1891, for example, he called on traditionalists to oppose a bill designed to protect child-brides by raising the minimum age at which their marriages could be consummated from ten to twelve years. In 1897, when bubonic plague devastated Poona, his political base, he violently attacked British measures to segregate possible victims in camps and appeared to advocate assassination as a legitimate political weapon. A few days later, two of his followers shot a British official and an army lieutenant as they were returning from a dinner party in celebration of Queen Victoria's diamond jubilee. Tilak had no direct connection with the murders, but he received an eighteen-month prison sentence for seditious conspiracy.

Despite the wide differences between the ultimate aims of the moderates and extremists, the Indian National Congress held together because both factions agreed on many immediate issues—in particular, the failure of the government not only to

advance the material prosperity of the mass of Indians but also to provide effective relief measures against famine and plague, which resulted in an absolute decline in population between 1895 and 1905. Some 25 percent of the government's total annual expenditure was spent on maintaining the administrative machine, especially its revenue arm. Almost one-third of public expenditure went for the army, which was engaged in wasteful frontier wars right up to the turn of the century. Much money was also swallowed up by the rail network, which was expanded largely to meet military needs. The capital for railroad construction was raised in London, but the interest had to be paid by Indian taxpayers. To many Congress members, it seemed that Britain was interested only in exploiting India for its own benefit.

Discontent boiled over during the reign of Lord Curzon, viceroy from 1898 to 1905. His term of office began promisingly enough: Well informed and immensely hardworking, he threw himself into a comprehensive overhaul of the administration, streamlining the bureaucracy and reforming the police service, and he pacified the North-West Frontier by turning it into a province policed mainly by its own Pathan tribes. Working up to fourteen hours a day, he personally oversaw the work of every department. Under his energetic command, more than 6,000 miles of track were added to the rail network and the area under irrigation was increased by almost 10 million acres. Shocked to find that India's ancient monuments were crumbling into ruin, he launched a program for their conservation.

Indian potentates process through Delhi during the durbar of 1903. A traditional Indian court ritual taken over by the British as a means of binding the loyalty of the Indian princes, the durbar was meticulously planned by the viceroy, Lord Curzon (above), as a celebration of imperialist ideals. Curzon even forbade the singing of a particular hymn because it contained an inappropriate reminder that kingdoms "may rise and wane."

But Curzon's administrative flair disguised a basic lack of political judgment. A dedicated imperialist, he believed that the British had come to India by "the decree of Providence, for the lasting benefit of millions of the human race"; and in common with perhaps most of the British, he perceived India as an unchanging society over which British rule would remain unchallenged as long as its representatives took care not to offend the princes and the traditional Indian upper classes. Such attitudes blinded Curzon to real shifts that were taking place. He underestimated the power of the educated middle classes, and the increasing appeal of their message of protest to other sectors of the Indian population. In Bombay and Bengal, where the cotton and jute textile industries were rapidly developing, entrepreneurs were also beginning to resent the injustices of British rule, and their factories were spawning a new class of industrial workers. Revivalist religious organizations had begun to appear, in which fundamentalist faith was mixed with political aspirations. And disaffected young people had begun to form secret terrorist societies, taking their cue from their imprisoned exemplar, Bal Gangadhar Tilak.

In 1904, Curzon sent a military expedition to Lhasa, the capital of Tibet, and in defiance of British government instructions, he forced the Tibetans to accept a British agent on their soil. To the Indians it looked as though the British intended using their country's revenues to achieve domination over all of Asia. Curzon's proposals to bring universities and private colleges under strict government control were interpreted by the Indians as attempts to restrict educational opportunities and thus stifle the growth of nationalism. By the time Curzon began his second term of office in 1905, his popularity had worn thin; within months, disapproval had turned to fury.

The flash point was Bengal. With a population of some 80 million and an area of more than 190,000 square miles, it was too large for one governor to rule efficiently. Without consulting Indian opinion, Curzon decided to partition the province, combining three populous districts of eastern Bengal with Assam to form the new province of East Bengal and Assam, with its capital at Dacca. Curzon proposed the partition on the grounds of administrative efficiency, but he was also aware of political advantages. As one of his predecessor's officials had written: "Bengal united is a power. Bengal divided will pull several different ways. . . . One of our main objects is to split up and thereby weaken a solid body of opponents to our rule."

Divide and rule is exactly how the policy looked to Bengal's predominantly Hindu middle class, the leaders of Indian nationalism. The new province would have a majority of uneducated Muslims, while in the rump of West Bengal, Hindus would be outnumbered by non-Bengali speakers. Gokhale, president of the Indian National Congress (whose annual meetings were now attended by more than 1,000 delegates) attacked the scheme as a "complete illustration of the worst features of the present system of bureaucratic rule—its utter contempt for public opinion, its arrogant pretensions to superior wisdom, its reckless disregard of the most cherished feelings of the people."

Unmoved, Curzon stated that partition would be "established with no great difficulty and with general consent." He was wrong. Led by Surendranath Banerjea (who came to be known as "Surrender Not"), Bengalis staged protest rallies and joined a campaign to boycott British goods, especially cotton, and promote Indian-made products. The campaign proved so effective that by 1908 imports were down more than 25 percent, and India's mills and looms were working flat out to meet the demand for home-produced cloth. For the first time, Congress had shown that it could command popular backing and organize effective actions against British rule.

Nor was the protest limited to nonviolent activities. From 1906, the terrorist societies began to put their beliefs into practice. Two attempts were made on the life of the lieutenant governor of Bengal, and in 1908, two Englishwomen were killed by a bomb intended for a British magistrate. Momentum was building, and the British were beginning to face a challenge to which their administration, grown hidebound over the years, lacked the flexibility to respond.

The raj would last for another four decades, but it was already clear to many that it was entering its final phase. British rule had not been wholly injurious: In the nineteenth century, India had been provided with a range of material benefits from railroads and irrigation systems to schools and hospitals; and the British administration of justice, while far from perfect, had brought peace and stability to many millions of their subjects. But the more perceptive British administrators had known all along that their rule could not last, and that this was as it should be. In 1838, Charles Trevelyan had written: "The existing connection, between two such distant countries as England and India, cannot in the nature of things be permanent; no effort of policy can prevent the natives from ultimately regaining their independence." By their endeavors, the British were able to reshape but not contain India; and when the mold of imperialism became hard and brittle, the raj would crack and break apart.

In Paris in 1900, crowds marvel at the incandescent display from the Palace of Electricity.

For the thriving industrial world of the late-nineteenth century, progress was bathed in the hard brilliance of electric light. Blazing from theatrical arc lamps, flooding sports arenas, sustaining lighthouses, illuminating parliamentary debates, and adding prestige and glamour to department stores and private homes, electricity brought a new power into people's lives that held the promise of changing the world in ways hitherto undreamed of.

The phenomenon of static electricity had long been recognized, but the task of producing continuous electric current taxed the ingenuity of scientists in all the industrialized nations. Building on previous discoveries that had established a connection between magnetism and electricity, the British scientist Michael Faraday was able in 1831 to demonstrate the principle of electromagnetic induction, in which the movement of a metal conductor through a magnetic field generates an electrical pulse. By 1850, several nations were manufacturing simple generators capable of transforming mechanical energy into electric current, and in the 1860s, Ernst Werner von Siemens in Germany developed a practical dynamo.

Taking up the challenge, the American inventor Thomas Alva Edison patented 225 new devices between 1879 and 1882—bulbs, fuses, sockets, switches, circuit breakers, and meters. By the end of the century, the United States had become the world leader in electrical development.

In 1900, when France held a great exhibition in Paris, the drama of the whole event depended upon the newly harnessed force. A commentator wrote: "Without electricity, the exhibition is merely an inert mass devoid of the slightest breath of life. . . . A single touch of the finger on a switch and the magic fluid pours forth. Everywhere the soul of the Palace of Electricity brings light and life."

A BLAZE OF PROGRESS

PUTTING POWER ON LINE

Before a commercial electric industry could be established, the problems of producing a reliable supply of electricity and distributing it to users had to be overcome. Early power stations depended on a flow of fast-moving water, but after 1884, efficient steam turbines using fossil fuels could produce the mechanical energy required to power the generator.

The first limited lighting systems used their own generators on the spot, but once methods had been developed of generating sufficient voltages for long-distance distribution, power stations moved out of town and cables proliferated to carry the current to the ever-growing number of consumers.

Seated calmly beneath the fulminations of a 12-million-volt discharge, Nikola Tesla, a gifted collaborator of Thomas Edison's, conducts an experiment into ultrahigh voltages in the United States.

Spun precariously between a forest of poles, a web of overhead telephone wires barely survives a blizzard in New York City in 1888 *(above)*. Edison, convinced that underground cables were the only safe method of distribution, trained his technicians to lay conduits under the streets *(right)*.

Ranks of gleaming steam turbines power the generators at Forth Banks at Newcastle upon Tyne, England, in 1892.

Painted by Louis Sontag in 1895, the Bowery district of New York City pulsates with life as blazing electric lights banish the darkness from the crowded sidewalks. The trolleys running down the middle of the street were electrified in 1899.

SETTING THE NIGHT ALIGHT

The earliest and most eye-catching of the transformations brought about by the newly available power was the lighting of streets, theaters, and homes. The first arc lamps, in which a current leaped in an arc across the gap between two carbon rods, gave off a light that was too brilliant for comfortable domestic use, but yielded dramatic effects out-of-doors—"like half a dozen harvest moons shining at once in the Strand," remarked a contemporary Londoner. The subsequent perfection of incandescent lamps, in which a filament was made to glow by passing a current through it, provided clean, convenient lighting that shed fashionable credit upon those who could afford to install it.

At the International Electrical Exhibition held in Frankfurt in 1891, a variety of glamorous light fixtures go on display to tempt aspiring users.

Four incandescent light bulbs show the variety of shapes developed after the prototype models invented by Thomas Edison in the United States and Joseph Swan in England in 1879. From left to right: a Swan lamp on a metal frame; an 1880 lamp with a filament of bamboo, one of Edison's preferred materials; a lamp with two filaments connected in series for use with high voltage; an 1890 bulb with a screw cap devised by Edison.

This old-world image was received in Paris after being transmitted from Marseilles by electric telegraph in 1863.

An ambitious array of domestic appliances for sale or rent is advertised in a catalog issued in 1894 by the City of London Electricity Supply Company, which sought to increase daytime domestic demand.

An 1883 drawing by the French satirist Albert Robida illustrates a fantasy that was soon to become reality: images and sound transmitted directly into the homes of viewers.

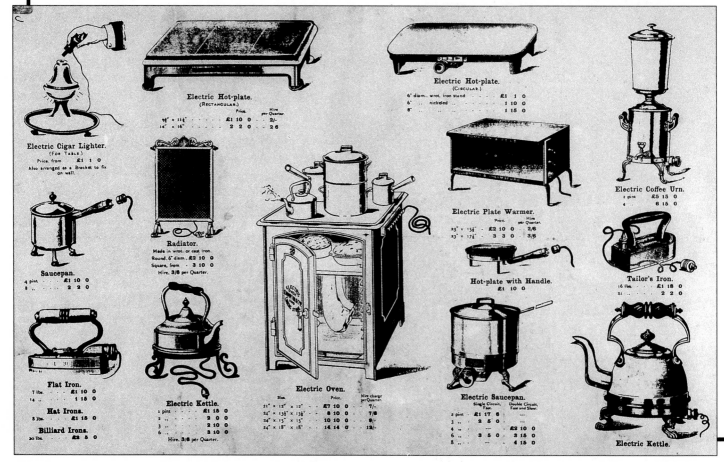

A RESOURCE FOR THE FUTURE

At the Paris Electrical Exhibition in 1881, visitors enjoy a vertical ride in an electric elevator developed for use in apartment buildings and department stores by Siemens, the first company to produce large-scale electric motors capable of powering trolleys, elevators, and machinery for industry.

Clean, silent, and reliable, electricity proved the springboard for a second industrial revolution, as a host of inventors sought to multiply its applications. Early devices were not without their hazards: The control panel for one electric stove in the 1890s, for example, was sternly labeled "Servants must be warned not to douse water upon these switches no matter what the provocation." But the ceaseless quest for convenience in the home—in addition to communication, transportation, and speculative ideas for future inventions, some of them justified by later discoveries—took the electrical industry into the twentieth century on a strong upward curve.

An Offord Electrocar goes through its limited paces in 1896. Though clean and quiet, electric automobiles lacked the speed and range to compete with gasoline-powered vehicles.

GERMANY'S IRON CHANCELLOR

"Long live His Imperial Majesty, the Emperor William." Ringing through the Hall of Mirrors in the palace of Versailles, twelve miles outside Paris, these words announced the accession on January 18, 1871, of the first ruler of a newly united Germany. Aroused from their reverent silence, the 600 assembled guests—princes, dukes and grand dukes, generals, ministers and diplomats—caught up the cry. "A thundering cheer, repeated at least six times, thrilled through the room," wrote Crown Prince Frederick in his diary, "while the flags and standards waved over the head of the new emperor of Germany."

The previous emperor had relinquished his crown in 1806, and his dominion, the Holy Roman Empire, had ceased to be a coherent political structure at least two centuries before. What had forged the various German-speaking lands into a new empire had been the momentum of war—culminating in the defeat of France and the occupation of Paris by a German army in 1870—and the pressure of economic necessity. Above all, however, it was the result of the will power and political skill of the tall, heavily built man with a drooping gray mustache, dressed in the uniform of a Prussian major general, who stood alone in front of the massed ranks of dignitaries in the Hall of Mirrors.

As the coronation ceremony drew to a close, Emperor William appeared not to notice this imposing figure but brushed past him to greet other officers on his way out of the hall. Otto von Bismarck was not in the least offended; to have achieved his ambition was reward enough. He had dominated German politics for nearly a decade, enforcing his will by an irresistible combination of charm, intellect, and rage, and he was to continue to do so for another twenty years.

Bismarck himself forever denied the importance of his personal influence: "Man can neither create nor direct the stream of time," he was to write after his retirement. "He can only travel upon it and steer with more or less skill and experience." But Bismarck proved to be the most skilled helmsman in Europe, and neither those who prospered nor those who suffered as a result of his aggressive policies shared his modest opinion of his own achievement.

In the 1840s, the lands of the German-speaking peoples comprised a mosaic of thirty-nine separate states, ranging from great kingdoms and principalities to minuscule dukedoms and archdukedoms whose imposing names disguised their lack of political significance. The two giants in this complex medley were Austria and Prussia, which were themselves made up of diverse territories. The far-flung Hapsburg empire of Austria ruled over a score of nationalities, including large numbers of Bohemian Czechs, Hungarian Magyars, and Italians in Lombardy and other northern provinces of Italy. The kingdom of Prussia consisted of two separate parts. One

This portrait of Otto von Bismarck, prime minister of Prussia from 1862 to 1890 and chancellor of Germany from 1871, captures the iron determination with which he transformed a patchwork of backward territories into the most powerful state in Europe. A skillful opportunist, he used both war and diplomacy to achieve his goal of a united Germany.

region, including the Prussian capital Berlin, stretched eastward along the Baltic Sea, incorporating what is now northwest Poland and including the port of Gdańsk; a southern spur took in the mineral-rich district of Silesia. Western Prussia, bordering the Rhine River and comprising provinces in Westphalia and the Rhineland, was a much smaller area, but it contained rich coal fields that were destined to play a major role in Germany's industrial revolution.

At the conclusion of the Napoleonic Wars in 1815, the Congress of Vienna had attempted to impose order on this miscellany by forming the German Confederation, a political league whose borders encompassed most of Austria and Prussia as well as the other German lands. Each one of the states sent delegates to an assembly, the Federal Diet, which met in Frankfurt under the presidency of Austria. The confederation was intended to act as the cement that would keep the pieces of central Europe from falling apart; under the guidance of Austria's ultraconservative statesman Prince Klemens Metternich, it effectively stifled all revolutionary tendencies within its member states.

In particular, Metternich was concerned with clamping down on nationalist movements, which he rightly identified with liberalism and viewed as threats to the established order. His task was made easier by the fact that most central European peoples were still largely illiterate and were unconcerned either with the preservation

Harnessing the military and industrial power of his native state of Prussia to his expansionist designs, Bismarck brought the German states north of the Main River into the North German Confederation in 1866. Five years later, the states south of the river joined the federation to create the unified German empire *(shaded yellow on the map below)*. Austria, distracted by rebellions and lagging behind the economic prosperity of Prussia, was powerless to prevent the steady accumulation of power by its ancient rival.

of their local cultures or with the establishment of independent states. In Austria, for example, the aspirations of the Bohemian Czechs and the Hungarians were limited to autonomy within the empire. In Prussia, a rigidly conservative society in which love of country was among the principal values a child learned at school, a deeply ingrained loyalty to the Hohenzollern dynasty appeared to rule out any possiblity of Pan-German nationalism.

Prussia was an agrarian country in which only a quarter of the population lived in towns of more than 2,000 citizens. Royal authority was transmitted by the hereditary nobility, the Junkers, who held all the high positions in the army and the bureaucracy. In the early decades of the nineteenth century, there existed between the Junkers and the peasantry a small but growing educated middle class, but any hopes that they might have articulated for political reform were stifled by rigid censorship and an efficient police system.

Toward the middle of the century, however, this age-old order of society began to change. In 1818, Prussia had initiated a commercial union, the Zollverein, which by 1834 embraced nearly all the German states, with the conspicuous exception of Austria. By promoting trade treaties, a common currency, and other benefits among its member states, the Zollverein stimulated rapid economic growth. Agricultural output increased, and emerging industries in the cities began to replace traditional craft workshops. Spurred by economic modernization, Prussia, along with most other countries in northern Europe, was entering a new age.

In 1848, Europe's peace was rudely shattered by a wave of revolutions. In Paris, King Louis-Philippe shaved off his whiskers, disguised himself with spectacles, and escaped to England, where he was joined by Austria's Prince Metternich. Emperor Ferdinand of Austria, fearing that a mob of students was about to occupy his palace, fled from Vienna. King Frederick William IV of Prussia allowed his capital to be occupied by liberal reformers; and the Federal Diet of the German Confederation gave way to a new body, the Frankfurt Parliament, whose members began work on a constitution for a united Germany.

Club-wielding police break up a radical demonstration in Berlin, the capital of Prussia, in 1848. This illustration was published in a broadsheet issued by liberal reformers who sought a written constitution for their country. In March, King Frederick William acceded to their demands and wept openly as the victims of clashes between the citizens and the authorities were carried in procession in front of his palace. But the following November, after uprisings against conservative regimes throughout Europe had been crushed, he allowed the Prussian army to regain control of the city.

Good intentions were not enough. A powerful undertow of reaction—and the ominous advance of a Russian army—restored the old order with almost as much speed, but considerably more bloodshed, as the unexpected wave that had knocked it off its feet. In France a short-lived republican government came under the control of Louis-Napoleon, great-nephew of Napoleon Bonaparte, who was soon to assume the imperial title of Napoleon III. A ferocious assault on Vienna restored the Hapsburg dynasty to the throne of the Austrian empire. The reformers in Berlin, divided among themselves, gradually allowed the Prussian army to reassert control. In the background loomed the Russian armies of Czar Nicholas I, which had crushed a rebellion in Poland and were moving into Hungary. "We live," wrote a Prussian nervously, "in the western provinces of the Russian empire."

Resuming his interrupted reign, Frederick William of Prussia rewarded the Junkers—who had remained unshaken by the tremors of revolution—with large tax concessions and government grants. At the same time, however, as if to compensate for the failed reform movement, Frederick William presented his subjects with a new constitution. It was by no means a liberal document; the king could still overrule any of the rights he promised his people. But there was now an elected parliament,

entitled to debate official policy and to vote on the budget, a privilege that would influence the course of German history.

Meanwhile, the members of the Frankfurt Parliament—who still sought to rally all the German-speaking people of Europe under a single constitutional monarchy—offered the crown of a united Germany to Frederick William. He scornfully refused. It was not in their power to offer him a title, the king replied, privately shuddering at the thought of being so elevated "by grace of bakers and butchers." Following Prussia's lead, the other major German states withdrew their support from the Frankfurt Parliament. Germany's optimistic attempt at unity had died after only a little more than a year of life.

Prussia now attempted to take the lead in German affairs by establishing a new federal parliament based in Erfurt. In response, Austria reconvened the Federal Diet in Frankfurt, and for a few weeks it appeared that Austria and Prussia might go to war. But Frederick William was not ready to fight the empire that for centuries had dominated central Europe. In December 1850, humbled and resentful, Prussia agreed by the Treaty of Olmütz to reassume its membership in the German Confederation.

Nothing had apparently altered, yet the stressful years of 1848 through 1850 had weakened the old order with myriad unseen fractures. Radical and liberal voices in the German-speaking states were quieter now, but they still called for an end to the multiplicity of borders and political systems that divided them. And the balance of power was steadily shifting.

After 1848, Austria was increasingly preoccupied with its Hapsburg domains and neglected its relations with the other German states. Rebellions in Hungary and northern Italy were defeated with difficulty in 1849, but large armies of occupation had to be maintained in these territories for years to come. The Austrian army itself, though still an impressive sight on the parade ground, was equipped with old-fashioned weapons and led by officers who owed their commissions to family connections rather than merit. The finances of the empire were in disorder. Deliberately excluded from the Zollverein by Prussia, Austria could only look on enviously at the economic progress now being made by its northern rival.

In the Ruhr valley, Prussia possessed the largest coal fields in Europe, and industrial development proceeded apace. Between 1848 and 1857, coal production more than doubled, and pig iron output rose 250 percent. To service its new industries, Prussia hastened to expand its railway network. But this was only partly for the moving of goods and the convenience of the public. Conscious that Prussia's far-flung territory, which bordered the Russian, French, and Austrian empires, was vulnerable to attack, military strategists urged the construction of railroads to facilitate the rapid mobilization of troops and transport of equipment. "A few million on the completion of our railways is far more profitably employed than on our new fortresses," wrote General Helmuth von Moltke, who became chief of the Prussian general staff in 1858.

No state in Europe venerated its army more than Prussia did. A century earli-

At the front of a group of army officers *(left)*, King William I and his chief of staff, General von Moltke, observe military maneuvers. A gifted but taciturn linguist and writer, Moltke was once described as being "silent in seven languages." Realizing that the use of railroads was about to transform the conduct of war, enabling large numbers of troops to be rapidly mobilized and supplied, Moltke fashioned the Prussian army into the most efficient fighting force in Europe, coordinated by a staff of trained tacticians and equipped with breech-loading light field guns *(below)*.

er, Frederick the Great had humbled Austria in the Seven Years' War, establishing Prussia as the greatest military power on the continent. Since its defeat by Napoleon in 1806, Prussia had been anxious to regain its military preeminence, and on the technical front, considerable progress had been made. New developments in engineering and metallurgy had given Prussia some of the most advanced weaponry in Europe, notably the Dreyse needle gun, so called because of its pointed firing pin. With its grooved, or rifled, barrel, this gun was considerably more accurate than the smooth-bored muskets still in use throughout much of Europe; and because it was loaded through the breech rather than the muzzle, its firing rate was faster.

In manpower and training, however, the army had not kept pace. While the population of Prussia had increased from 11 to 18 million, the annual intake of army recruits had remained unchanged. As relations with Austria grew increasingly chilly, and as a new French empire became established to the west, Prussia's need to reorganize its armed forces became ever more urgent.

According to the existing system, soldiers served for five years in the national army and then joined the Landwehr, a reserve militia that could be called upon in emergencies. Liberal politicians considered the Landwehr an important means of involving the Prussian people in the defense of the nation. The Junkers, on the other hand, were contemptuous of the Landwehr and its middle-class officers, and in 1858 they gained a powerful ally. King Frederick William had long been mentally unstable; now he grew incurably mad, and his sixty-one-year-old younger brother, Prince William, was proclaimed regent, king in all but name. A simple, old-fashioned Prussian who had devoted his life to the army, William despised the "dirty militiamen" of the Landwehr, and he put forward proposals to increase the military budget and the size of the standing army. He also demanded lengthening the term of service in the national army.

This last condition proved unacceptable to Prussia's elected lower chamber, whose members feared for the continued existence of the Landwehr. Faced with an obstinate ruler surrounded by a clique of ultraconservative Junkers, the politicians exercised their one effective power and declined to authorize the new military budget for more than a year at a time.

The dispute dragged on. In 1861, William became king on his brother's death, and his advisers began to advocate a military coup to rid the country of all liberal opposition. William, while adamantly opposed to popular rule, nevertheless refused to contemplate a violent solution to Prussia's dilemma. He offered instead to abdicate. This would have left the throne open to his liberal-leaning son Frederick, who would doubtless accede to the demands of the elected lower chamber. Desperate to have their way and still maintain the present king in power, William's military advisers played their last card, one they had not used before because they themselves feared its consequences. In September 1862, the minister of war sent an urgent telegram to Otto von Bismarck, the Prussian ambassador in Paris. *"Periculum in mora. Dépêchez-vous!"* read this message. "Delay is dangerous. Hurry!"

Bismarck had entered politics only by chance. He was born in 1815 on an estate fifty miles west of Berlin; his father was a Junker and his mother the daughter of an influential civil servant. He studied law at Göttingen University in the kingdom of Hanover, and after a brief spell in the civil service, which he loathed, he returned to the family estate for eight fallow years, during which he gained a local reputation as a hard-drinking, fast-riding womanizer. In 1847, he attended a national meeting of provincial assemblies as a substitute member of his local delegation and owed his first chance to speak in public to the retirement of a permanent member. But his oratory made an immediate impression: He delivered his speeches in an insistent high-pitched voice, attacking with lacerating eloquence any proposals in which he detected a hint of liberalism. In 1851, Bismarck was appointed chief Prussian delegate to the German Confederation in Frankfurt. He had no diplomatic experience; God, he said, would give him understanding.

In Frankfurt, Bismarck took up the cudgel of the Prussian nationalists, fiercely opposing Austria's every move. Upon discovering that by tradition only the Austrian delegate smoked during meetings, Bismarck aggressively puffed away at Havana cigars. On a more elevated level, he blocked Austria's admission to the Zollverein and shocked his superiors in Berlin with talk of a possible alliance with France and even of war. "Vienna's policy has made Germany suddenly too small for us both," he wrote to a military adviser in Berlin. "We shall be obliged sooner or later to fight Austria for our existence."

Bismarck believed that his was a realistic appraisal of the political situation, but others began to regard their outspoken delegate as a dangerous liability. "Red reactionary, smells of blood, only to be used when the bayonet rules," noted Frederick William. Upon coming to power as regent, Prince William appointed Bismarck ambassador to Russia, where it was felt that he would not be able to do much harm. Three years later, as the military budget crisis deepened, he was transferred to Paris. But there were many in Berlin who felt that only Bismarck had the strength and the skill to resolve the dispute between king and parliament that threatened to plunge Prussia into civil war.

Recalled to Berlin, Bismarck's first task was to persuade the king that he could, in fact, save the country. William was no admirer of Bismarck's reckless words and policies; his wife, Queen Augusta, loathed the man. Yet so great was Bismarck's force of character, and so beguiling his manner, that after a single interview at the king's summer palace outside Berlin, William tore up his letter of abdication. It was as prime minister of Prussia that Bismarck left the palace.

Bismarck went to war against parliament with characteristic gusto, demanding immediate approval for an increase in military funds. It was imperative that Prussia be strong because power alone would solve Germany's problems, he warned, ending his speech with a chilling prophecy: "Not by speeches and majorities will the great questions of the day be decided—that was the mistake of 1848 and 1849—but by iron and blood."

When the liberals refused to budge in their opposition to William's army reforms, Bismarck simply took the necessary money without authorization. Since no provision was made in the constitution to resolve a stalemate between monarch and parliament, he argued, the king as head of state must be entitled to have his way. More bluntly Bismarck explained, "Whoever has power in his hands then proceeds according to his will."

Liberal politicians were enraged, but memories of defeat in 1848 were still fresh. Besides, a number of them had begun to discover a sneaking admiration for this overbearing prime minister. If there was any one issue that united the people of Prussia, it was a burning nationalism; and for all Bismarck's antidemocratic maneuvers over the budget, he had proved that he knew how to antagonize the Austrians.

Some might still believe that Prussia and Austria could share power in a German confederation. For the militants, however, only a Prussian-dominated union of German states north of the Main River would suffice.

Bismarck had long shared this view. He also knew that as long as there was a common enemy threatening the nation from without, domestic problems would take second place. Accordingly, he continued to exclude Austria from the Zollverein, then rubbed salt in the wound by establishing a trading agreement with France. He also reduced the possibility of Russian support for Austria by siding with Czar Alexander against a Polish nationalist uprising.

Austria made one last effort to assert its power over Prussia. In 1863, Emperor Francis Joseph summoned a meeting of all the German princes to revise the constitution of the German Confederation and sent the king of Saxony to bear a personal invitation to William of Prussia. Bismarck persuaded his king to reject the invitation.

ITALY RESURGENT

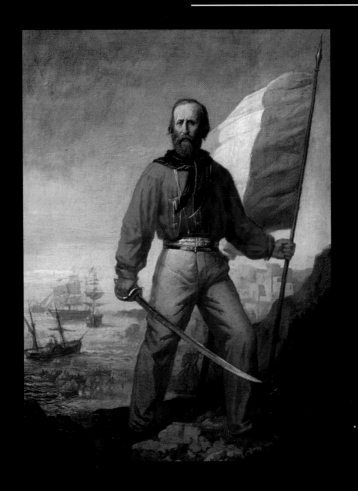

German calls for unification were echoed on the opposite side of the Alps within the divided states of Italy, where the Risorgimento—literally, "resurgence"—movement sought to throw off the yoke of foreign rule. In the north, Count Camillo di Cavour, prime minister of the independent kingdom of Piedmont-Sardinia, ousted the Austrians from Lombardy in 1859 with the aid of French troops. Tuscany and other northern states voted for unity with Piedmont. In the south, Sicily was liberated from the rule of the Bourbon king of Naples by the revolutionary commander Giuseppe Garibaldi, whose landing on the coast with 1,000 red-shirted volunteers in May 1860 is shown in the painting on the left. Advancing to the mainland, Garibaldi met up with the troops of Piedmont-Sardinia, which had swept down through the Papal states. He greeted their monarch, Victor Emmanuel II, with the words: "I salute the first king of Italy." Complete unification was achieved in 1870 with the annexation of Rome, after French troops guarding the papacy had been withdrawn at the beginning of the Franco-Prussian War.

Here was a ploy, he was convinced, to assimilate Prussia and its army into an Austrian-dominated Germany.

While hostility simmered between them, Prussia and Austria unexpectedly became allies. In 1863, King Christian IX of Denmark declared that the duchy of Schleswig, to the south of the Danish peninsula, was a part of the Danish state. The kings of Denmark had long been nominal overlords of both Schleswig and its southern neighbor, Holstein. But the population of these territories was predominantly German-speaking, and Christian's declaration provoked widespread anger. With the tide of nationalism running so strong, Bismarck was in no position to delay Prussian intervention. Austria, for its part, could not leave Prussia to solve the problem alone, increasing its prestige and possibly its territory. So the unlikely alliance was formed. Bismarck, always an opportunist, prepared to exploit the advantage as it came.

The Danes were easily crushed, and the Treaty of Vienna, ratified in October 1864, gave Prussia and Austria joint dominion over Schleswig and Holstein. By now, however, Bismarck had assessed that the time was ripe for a complete rupture with Prussia's powerful southern rival, and during the next two years he sought to isolate Austria by means of agreements with France and Italy. France gave a vague assurance of neutrality; Italy promised to attack Austria if Prussia did so within three months. Provoked beyond endurance, Austria took its case to the German diet in Frankfurt and urged the federation to mobilize against Prussia.

The war between Austria and Prussia was as decisive as it was short. Prussia was spoiling for battle, and after four years of unconstitutional funding, Moltke's military machine was ready to demonstrate its effectiveness. Most of the smaller German states allied themselves with Austria, but they played little part in the conflict. By the end of June, Prussia had crushed all resistance in Hanover, Hesse, and Saxony. Bavaria and its southern neighbors offered Austria nothing more than moral support. When the Prussian army, advancing in three columns, converged upon the village of Sadova, fifty miles across the Austrian border, it was the Hapsburg army alone that it faced.

On July 3, 1866, nearly half a million men met in battle in the rain-sodden woods and fields around Sadova to decide the future of their two nations. Bismarck and King William observed the fighting together, sitting side by side on horseback for thirteen hours; the king was nominal commander in chief of the army, and Bismarck, who had once been a lieutenant in the reserves, wore a Prussian spiked helmet and the uniform of a major general.

The Austrians fought doggedly to the end, losing 10,000 men in twenty minutes in one final assault. But the Prussians, whose breech-loading rifles could outfire the Austrians' weapons at a rate of five to one, finally outmaneuvered and outgunned their enemy. Bismarck was distressed by what he saw. "If foreign ministers had always followed their sovereigns to the front, history would have fewer wars to tell of," he later remarked. But nothing could conceal his glee in the victory. "I have beaten them all! All!" he exulted soon after the battle, pounding on a table.

An air of euphoria swept over Prussia. Only a handful of critics dared to question the wisdom of Bismarck's war against Austria. Liberals who had railed against his authoritarian rule, and conservatives who had suspected his loyalty to the monarchy, now raised their voices in Bismarck's praise. A doting parliament voted to legalize Bismarck's appropriation of funds for military reform retroactively, and as a bonus they granted him a massive reward. Bismarck used the money to buy a 14,825-acre

estate at Varzin in Pomerania; it became a place of retreat and, with its paper mill and distillery, a source of considerable private income.

The king and his generals, exhilarated with victory, were eventually persuaded by Bismarck to moderate their terms of peace. France and Russia would not tolerate the Prussian annexation of substantial parts of the Austrian empire, he argued. But the Seven Weeks' War—as it became known—ended forever the old German Confederation. Austria established a dual monarchy with Hungary and, by the Treaty of Prague, agreed to recognize "a new form of Germany without participation of the Austrian empire." Prussia annexed the province of Schleswig and formed a bridge between its eastern and western

Victorious German troops swarm over the ruins of Fort Issey, outside the walls of Paris, at the end of the Franco-Prussian War in 1871. During the four-month siege of the French capital, starving citizens in the city—as shown in a cartoon from a French newspaper *(inset)*—were reduced to hunting for sewer rats to eat.

territories by assimilating Hanover and three smaller states that had allied themselves with Austria. For the time being, the German states south of the Main River were allowed to maintain "an internationally independent existence" as a buffer zone between Prussia and France.

The North German Confederation created by Bismarck's victory in 1866 consisted of twenty-two states, but it spoke with the voice of Prussia. Individual states maintained their own administration, but all foreign policy and military matters were under federal control. The constitution, written almost entirely by Bismarck, called for two houses: a federal council, the Bundesrat, and a popular assembly, the Reichstag. The members of the Bundesrat were diplomats appointed by each state; Prussia, by far the largest one, sent seventeen delegates, while Saxony, the second biggest, was represented by only four. Since a simple majority was all that was necessary to reach a decision, Prussia invariably had its way. The Reichstag was elected by universal manhood suffrage, and its members succeeded in securing a few powers that Bismarck had not originally intended. Control over military expenditure and foreign policy, however, continued to elude them.

The people may have had a voice, but Germany was in no way a democracy. The president of the confederation was the king of Prussia, and its chief minister, who was known as the federal chancellor, was the prime minister of Prussia. The signature of Bismarck was thus necessary to validate all laws.

Constitutional matters could not distract Bismarck for long from his overriding interest in international affairs. His most immediate cause for concern was the growth of strong patriotic and anti-Prussian feelings within France. Bismarck himself denied wanting a war with France, but Moltke and other prominent officers thirsted for a further display of German might. And there was, too, a good argument for provoking France into war. The southern German states of Bavaria, Baden, and Württemberg had signed defense pacts with Prussia in 1867, but they were resisting Prussian attempts to coax them into union with the North German Confederation. A war with France might provide the impetus to weld a disunited people together.

Bismarck may not have anticipated war with France in the spring of 1870, but he deliberately played with fire near his inflammable neighbor. In 1868, a revolution in Spain sent Queen Isabella II into exile, and in the following year the vacant throne was offered to the Hohenzollern Prince Leopold, who was distantly related to King William. Bismarck supported this proposal: As a Catholic, Leopold would be acceptable to Spain, while his German connection would ensure Prussia a friendly presence on the far side of France.

When the French foreign minister demanded an explanation of Prussia's involvement in the affair, William, reluctant to antagonize France any further, withdrew Leopold's candidacy, and the whole business might have ended there. The French ambassador, however, meeting the king in the resort town of Ems, demanded a pledge that Prussia would never again propose the Hohenzollern candidacy. William again repeated that the candidacy had been withdrawn, but he firmly declined to make any demeaning promise to France.

Throughout most of this crisis, Bismarck had been at his estate in Varzin, a six-

Rows of hospital beds occupied by wounded German soldiers line the Hall of Mirrors in the French royal palace of Versailles during the siege of Paris. Other rooms in the palace were occupied by William I of Prussia and Bismarck, whose fare—in stark contrast to that of the hapless Parisians—included turtle soup, wild boar's head, and sauerkraut boiled in champagne.

hour journey from Berlin. When he arrived in the capital, he received by telegraph an account of King William's encounter with the French ambassador, and he saw his opportunity to take control of events. He edited and condensed the telegram, keeping to the facts but making it appear that the king had angrily dismissed the ambassador. Bismarck then instructed that the Ems Telegram, as it became known, be distributed to embassies and newspapers all over the Continent. "It will have the effect of a red flag on the Gallic bull," he proudly announced to General von Moltke. On the following day, France ordered the mobilization of its army. The Franco-Prussian War had begun.

The French troops were spirited and well armed: Their rifles had a far longer range than the German needle guns, and they also possessed an early form of machine gun, the *mitrailleuse*. But they were vastly outnumbered by the half million German troops who advanced into France in three separate columns. By the end of August, one French army was besieged in the town of Metz, and the other, led in person by Napoleon III, had become encircled in the town of Sedan near the Belgian border, 155 miles northeast of Paris.

On September 1, 1870, from a flat-topped hill amid the stubble of a farmer's field, William and his entourage watched the German troops steadily close in on the

THE PARIS COMMUNE: A DREAM SHATTERED

trapped French army. *"Ah, les pauvres gens!"*—"Ah, the unhappy people!"—the king was heard to sigh after one suicidal attempt by the French to break out. By midafternoon the big guns had fallen silent, and a French officer arrived with a brief message: "Since I was not able to die in the midst of my troops, it only remains for me to surrender my sword to the hands of Your Majesty. I am Your Majesty's good brother, Napoleon."

Two days later, in a cold drizzle, the French emperor departed from Sedan to spend the rest of his life in exile in England. More than 100,000 of his soldiers remained behind as prisoners of war.

But the French people stubbornly fought on. Encircled by the Germans, the citizens of Paris endured a bombardment of up to 400 shells a day. Many starved to death, and the wealthy were reduced to eating animals from the zoo. In the provinces, popular armies continued a makeshift campaign, and resistance fighters known as *franc-tireurs* goaded the Germans into savage acts of reprisal.

Bismarck, quartered with the king in the palace of Versailles, feared that the tide of public opinion might turn and persuade his south German allies to conclude a separate peace with France. Since a major incentive for the war had been unification with the southern states, he acted quickly to secure their permanent alliance.

It was not an easy task. Although Baden was eager to join an enlarged Germany, the kings of Bavaria and Württemberg were not. Bismarck granted them substantial political concessions and bribed Bavaria's extravagant King Ludwig with a secret pension, paying him with money that he had illegally sequestered after annexing the kingdom of Hanover.

Even King William, who took great pride in being sovereign of Prussia, was reluctant at first to accept the title of emperor, or *Kaiser,* of a united Germany. At last, however, the negotiations were complete. In January 1871, the coronation of King William in the Hall of Mirrors signaled the birth of the second Reich, a new German empire more united and more powerful than its distant predecessor, the Holy Roman Empire.

"The balance of power has been entirely destroyed," declared the British prime minister Benjamin Disraeli, referring to Germany's new dominance of the continent of Europe. Within Germany too, the balance had shifted. "The German nation errs if it thinks it will be able to put the rifle in one corner and turn to the arts and the happiness of peace," wrote the historian Jakob Burckhardt in 1871. "Iron and blood" was no longer a phrase to shock; it had become the orthodoxy of the empire.

Under pressure from his generals and the vengeful German public, Bismarck forced a harsh peace upon France. By the Treaty of Frankfurt, agreed in March 1871, the nation's eastern industrial provinces of Alsace and Lorraine were transferred to the new German empire. On top of this, Bismarck demanded a punitive indemnity that was calculated to cripple the French economy.

Within Germany, the federal constitution of 1867 smoothly evolved into the imperial constitution of 1871. Once again the Bundesrat was dominated by Prussia, and the Reichstag, although it contained many vociferous critics of Bismarck, was unwilling to mount a serious challenge to the man who had united Germany.

To the citizens of Paris, who for four months had heroically withstood the might of the German army, the French National Assembly's submission to the harsh peace terms dictated by Bismarck was a keen humiliation. They determined to make Paris a self-governing commune, and in March 1871, they voted into power a range of republican, socialist, and anarchist delegates.

In their programs to improve the lot of the working people, the Communards sought to revive the spirit of the French Revolution of 1789. A statue of Napoleon Bonaparte dressed in a Roman toga, a symbol of imperialism, was toppled from its pedestal *(left),* and the red flag of socialism was planted in its place. But hopes of inspiring a countrywide revolution were soon dashed. Under the orders of Louis-Adolphe Thiers, head of the provisional French government, troops entered Paris in May and proceeded to stamp out the commune with brutal ferocity. Some 20,000 citizens were slaughtered in a single week. Photographs such as the one shown here were used to identify activists.

Workers at an Essen factory founded by the Krupp family of German industrialists are dwarfed by a massive steam hammer, used for forging steel ingots. Alfred Krupp manufactured cast-steel railroad track and equipment, then turned to arms and ammunition for the Prussian army. After his death in 1887, his son Friedrich Alfred developed an alternating series of high-powered shells and supposedly impenetrable armors, which he sold to some thirty foreign governments.

William, reluctant to accede to some of his chancellor's demands, invariably backed down when Bismarck threatened to resign. "It is not easy to be emperor under such a chancellor," lamented the old monarch. But Bismarck, exhausted by war and bored by peace, became increasingly eccentric and irritable. He complained about a dozen conditions, from gout to varicose veins, all the while continuing to eat, drink, and smoke himself into a state of ever-greater illness. "They eat here always until the walls burst," wrote an astonished guest of Bismarck's household. Disraeli was equally amazed by the great man's gluttony. "Prince Bismarck," he wrote, "with one hand full of cherries and the other of shrimps, eaten alternately, complains he cannot sleep."

He had better things to do than sleep. "I have spent the whole night hating," he once remarked. Irascible and self-centered, he was infuriated by an outspoken group within the Reichstag known as the Center party, which had been established to protect the rights of German Catholics in the predominantly Protestant empire. Bismarck began to perceive the Catholic church and its German supporters as genuine

threats to the state. In 1870, Pope Pius IX had condemned nationalism as one of the "principal errors of our times." The Catholics, in Bismarck's view, were attempting to undermine the empire: "What we have here," he thundered, "is the age-old struggle for power between priest and king."

Hoping to exploit the deep-rooted prejudices of many German Protestants, Bismarck launched a Kulturkampf—a cultural struggle—against the Catholic church. New laws insisted upon civil marriage and upon state-appointed lay inspectors for all church schools. Priests were required henceforth to be licensed by the state before they could practice, monastic orders were banned, and hundreds of Catholics were exiled or imprisoned.

But Bismarck had misread the spirit of his people, many of whom were ashamed of the persecution of their fellow citizens. In the 1874 elections, the Center party gained a substantial number of seats. And in his attempts to implicate the French in an international Catholic conspiracy directed against Germany, Bismarck also misjudged the international situation. He had hoped that talk of war would bring the other great powers to exert a restraining pressure on France, which had now paid off the war indemnity and was channeling funds into building up its army. It was not France, however, that his neighbors now feared. In 1875, Russia and Britain insisted that the warmongering come to an end. Bismarck, who took lessons from others with very bad grace, resentfully complied.

As the Kulturkampf ran out of steam, a new enemy appeared. Bismarck loathed idealists of any kind, but he saw the growth of an international socialist movement as a particular threat to his autocratic rule. When the Social Democratic party emerged in 1875, Bismarck was determined to destroy it at birth. His first attempt to legislate against the socialists was blocked by the Reichstag: The majority party, the National Liberals, had eaten from Bismarck's hand for five years, but they still had enough courage to see that antisocialism laws might easily be used against any other critics of the Reich. But then fortune played into Bismarck's hands.

In May 1878, an unemployed plumber fired at the emperor, who was riding in his carriage in Berlin. Claiming that the plumber had once been a member of the Social Democratic party, Bismarck again sought to introduce antisocialist laws. The Reichstag stood firm, but just a week later William was severely wounded in a second attempt on his life.

"Now I've got the scoundrels," Bismarck gloated, undeterred by his failure to establish any link between this would-be assassin and the socialists, and he immediately dissolved the Reichstag. In the ensuing elections, the National Liberals lost nearly a quarter of their seats, and although the Social Democrats retained a token presence, the new assembly passed a range of repressive laws. These deprived socialist organizations of the right of assembly and publication, and they forbade various ill-defined activities including "endangering class harmony." The only blot on Bismarck's triumph was the Reichstag's insistence that the antisocialist laws be renewed every three years.

Bismarck next turned his attention to the faltering economy, a significant factor in the rise of socialism. In the years that followed Prussia's victory over France, currency reforms and the payment of the French war indemnity had brought huge amounts of new capital into Prussia. Much of this money was invested in industrial development and banking enterprises: 726 new joint-stock companies were formed between 1871 and 1873, compared with just 276 in the previous eighty years. Then, in 1873, accusations of corruption in high places were voiced in the Reichstag. Investors lost confidence, and when the Vienna stock exchange crashed in May, the Berlin Bourse followed it down.

Those who had lost their capital did not find it easy to recover, for all of Europe was descending into a long period of economic depression. Cheap imports from overseas—including Russian and American grain, and Australian wool and refrigerated meat—undercut domestic agriculture. Railway construction was slowed down, and the iron industry foundered with it. The house of Krupp, the largest industrial concern in Europe, laid off 1,800 workers and remained in business only by mortgaging all its property to the banks.

One disturbing outcome of this crisis was a rash of articles in the popular press that fostered the myth of a Jewish conspiracy against the German state. During the course of the century, many Jewish families had risen to prominence in business and artistic circles in Hamburg, Berlin, and Frankfurt; one of the best-known Jewish financiers, Gerson von Bleichröder, was Bismarck's personal banker. But they had not achieved complete integration into German society and were now cast as scapegoats for the nation's economic troubles.

Under pressure from wealthy industrialists and estate owners, Bismarck made an abrupt change in policy. After years of advocating free trade, he suddenly became a protectionist. "We have been slowly bleeding to death because of insufficient protection," he announced to the Reichstag in 1879. Breaking with the National Liberals, who were doctrinaire free traders, he bargained for support from the previously despised Center party and pushed through a package of tariffs and indirect taxes that greatly benefited the industrial and agricultural establishment. The Junkers, who had watched their economic power slipping away, once again supplied the nation's grain, while a series of purges in the civil service restored them to their traditional position of dominance. Scarcely any of their profits trickled down to the working classes, who continued to swell the ranks of the Social Democrats. As for the National Liberals, their reward for years of compromise was to be thrown out in the cold. Without Bismarck's patronage they failed to regain their powerful position in German politics.

Bismarck understood why so many workers were tempted by socialism; he even admitted a genuine sympathy for their plight. "I too am a socialist," he once observed to a surprised academic. What he meant by this cryptic statement was revealed in 1881, when he introduced a draft bill to insure workers against industrial accidents. Claiming that his aim was "to keep alive the sense of human dignity," he made no secret of his more immediate political purpose, which was "to create in the great mass of have-nots the conservative frame of mind." Determined to tame the discontented workers with state benefits, he pushed through a series of bills during the 1880s that introduced the first compulsory social security system in Europe. Socialists rightly saw this policy as a calculated tactic, rather than a genuine change of direction. They accepted the benefits but continued their opposition to the increasingly repressive government.

In his foreign policy, Bismarck forsook his old opportunist tactics and concentrated instead on securing continental peace by means of a complex web of formal treaties. In 1878, after a war in which Russia had defeated the Ottoman empire, Bismarck convened the Congress of Berlin and played the part of what he called "honest broker" between the powers who disputed Russia's gains. In the following year,

Schoolgirls pose for a photographer in their gymnastics class. Compulsory elementary education in the German empire increased literacy and contributed to the growth of industrial might, but an emphasis on discipline and obedience to authority reinforced the existing class structure. Women were not admitted to universities; one female student wrote that the purpose of her education had been solely to provide her husband "with a proper domestic atmosphere."

Bismarck negotiated the Dual Alliance with his old enemy Austria-Hungary, a partnership that was later extended to include Italy, and in 1881, he initiated the Dreikaiserbund, or Three Emperors' League, by which Germany, Austria-Hungary, and Russia agreed to remain neutral in the event that any one of them became involved in a war with a fourth great power. Bismarck's priorities were to guard against the threat of war on his own back doorstep, where both Russia and Austria-Hungary were eager to profit territorially from the decline of the Ottoman empire, and to protect Germany from the vengeful wrath of France, which was still licking its wounds after its defeat in 1871.

Preoccupied with maintaining the security of Germany within Europe, Bismarck was less interested in acquiring overseas possessions. Nonetheless, as the British and French empires became ever larger, he was anxious to bolster his standing in international diplomacy, and in 1884, he announced that Germany had taken under its protection various territories in which private companies or adventurers had established treaties and trading concessions. By this simple means, Germany acquired an overseas empire of more than 965,000 square miles, including extensive

In a portrait completed after his death, the vain and flamboyant Ludwig of Bavaria displays his fondness for theatrical costume and ornament.

A ceramic swan from the castle of Neuschwanstein—"New Swan Crag" —testifies to Ludwig's love of Wagner's opera *Lohengrin,* in which the knight of the swan rescues the heroine from her oppressor but then causes her death by his departure.

Indifferent to the rapid modernization of the German empire, King Ludwig II of Bavaria devoted much of his energy to acting out his romantic fantasies. His fascination with ancient Teutonic legends was excited by the composer Richard Wagner, whom he invited to Munich soon after his accession in 1864. While Wagner glorified German nationalism in operas that wove music, text, and character into an epic unity, Ludwig's own grandiose schemes were more self-indulgent: He built three imposing castles in a medley of architectural styles and made of their interiors a hermetic world of luxury and extravagance. Ludwig's eccentricities finally turned to madness, and in 1886 he drowned himself.

The giddy pinnacles of Neuschwanstein Castle in the Bavarian Alps embody Ludwig's fairy-tale version of the Middle Ages (left). Typical of the equally fantastic interior decoration is the mock-Byzantine splendor of the throne room (below).

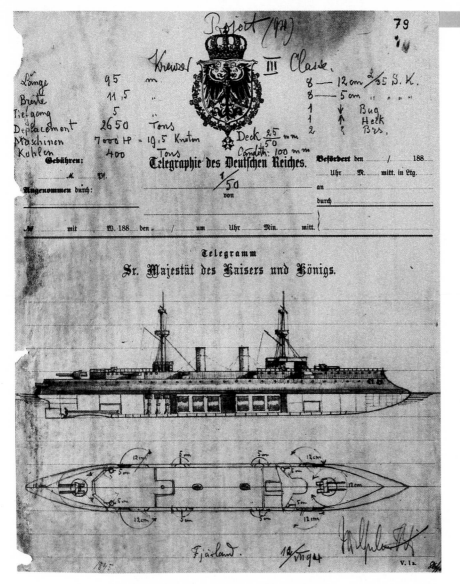

This blueprint for a battle cruiser was sketched on a blank telegraph form by Emperor William II of Germany in 1894. Although his own designs were deemed impracticable by professional naval architects, the emperor was determined that his nation should build a strong navy in order to challenge Great Britain's supremacy on the high seas.

domains in the African continent and a number of islands in the Pacific Ocean. Bismarck's intention that the colonies should be run by private chartered companies proved unworkable, and the burden of organizing these unprofitable ventures fell back on the state. Within five years, Bismarck had lost his appetite for foreign adventure: "I am not a colonial man," he declared in 1889.

For all Bismarck's skill in rearranging the pieces on the European chessboard, as he referred to it, he could not alleviate the problems that he faced at home. His domestic tactics had always been confrontational: In order to push through the laws that he wanted, he would invariably attempt to frighten the populace into his way of thinking. It was his attempt to renew the antisocialist laws by once again conjuring up the threat of a "red menace" that led to a fatal miscalculation.

On March 3, 1888, in a voice choked with emotion, Bismarck announced that Emperor William was dead. He had long dreaded the accession of the liberal Crown Prince Frederick and his strong-minded wife, the eldest child of Britain's Queen Victoria, but Frederick III reigned for only three months before his death from cancer of the throat. His son William, who was not yet thirty years old, now came to the throne. William II was vain, impulsive, and idealistic, and Bismarck was confident that he could control this emperor as he had controlled his grandfather before him.

Now nearly seventy-five years old, Bismarck was in better physical condition than he had been for many years. A young doctor had ensured that he exercised, slept well, and ate moderately; his weight had fallen from 250 to 195 pounds. Nor had he lost his political energy and daring. He recognized that his attempts to crush socialism with a combination of repressive laws and state welfare had met with only partial success, and that the elected politicians of the Reichstag would continue to oppose him. Therefore, he concluded, the constitution must be abolished. He would persuade William that the country was near rebellion; then he would take the law into his own hands, where he had always felt it belonged. There would be violence, but he had faced that before. "In the end you have to smash the crockery," he calmly remarked to an ambassador. "These questions . . . will not be solved without a blood bath, just as the question of German unity was not."

To Bismarck's amazement, the emperor refused to begin his reign with a civil war. William was sympathetic to the German workers, and he had no intention of turning guns upon them. As if in a dream, Bismarck realized that his time as chancellor was at an end. On March 18, 1890, he wrote to William: "It is very painful for me to terminate my accustomed relationship to the All Highest and to the political life of the Reich and Prussia."

No one opposed his departure. He retired to the country, where he lived for eight more years in bitterness and boredom, working on his memoirs. On Bismarck's

In a portrait painted in 1890, the year he forced the resignation of Chancellor Bismarck, Emperor William II strives to personify the Prussian ideal of the warrior-king, while hiding from view his stunted left arm, which had been damaged at birth. Commenting on the emperor's bombastic pose, a French general remarked: "That is not a portrait, it is a declaration of war."

eightieth birthday in 1895, the emperor paid a formal and uncomfortable visit, but an unforgiving Reichstag refused to extend their congratulations.

When Otto von Bismarck died in 1898, the German empire that he had created was twenty-seven years old, and its material strength and progress appeared sufficient answer to his critics. Even though there had been periodic economic depressions, industry had continued to grow. The mighty iron and steel works of the Ruhr, Silesia, and Saxony were the most productive in all of Europe. Germany's chemical industries dominated the world with a variety of products that ranged from synthetic dyes and drugs to explosives. No other European state produced so much electricity. The army had been expanded, and a powerful navy now sought to challenge Great Britain's dominion of the seas.

But German society had failed to attain a matching maturity. Politically, the empire was a complicated and unstable amalgam of the antiquated and the modern, a form of feudal capitalism in which the ruling elite of landowners and entrepreneurs was made anxious and insecure by the speed of their country's industrial progress and the growth of political aspirations among the laboring classes. Bismarck's determination to maintain the absolute authority of himself and the emperor had increased the tensions in society to the point where the only resolution he could propose had been dictatorship.

Dedicated to peace, Bismarck had repeatedly cowed the Reichstag by invoking an external threat, and after his retirement, the military continued to enjoy an exaggerated prestige. Civilians stepped off the pavement to let an officer pass by, while their fickle young emperor, besotted with his army, dressed himself in ever more theatrical military costumes. Both physically and spiritually, the nation was preparing for war, unable to relinquish the fiercely militaristic mood that Bismarck had harnessed and directed toward the goal of unification. Aroused by the labyrinth of political alliances and overlapping treaties that Bismarck had constructed, suspicion and enmity seethed beneath the brittle peace of Europe. In 1914, when that peace was finally shattered—by a conflict in the Balkans, as Bismarck had feared—the seeds had long been planted for the grim harvest of the twentieth century.

FEEDING THE MULTITUDES

By the middle of the nineteenth century, a declining death rate and, probably, an increasing birthrate in industrial Europe and America had begun to pose the severe problem of an ever-increasing number of hungry mouths demanding to be fed. The population of Europe, which by 1800 had reached around 187 million, was to more than double by the end of the century. That of the United States, boosted by waves of immigrants, rose from 17 million in 1840 to 76 million in 1900. The crisis was especially acute in cities, into which a large proportion of these extra souls poured.

Science and industrial technology, which had themselves been largely responsible for improving living conditions and life expectancies, provided many of the urgently needed solutions. Age-old patterns of subsistence agriculture were transformed by the introduction of machines such as Cyrus McCormick's mechanical reaper, shown above, which could do the work of five scythe-wielding farm hands. Advances in stockbreeding improved both the quality

and quantity of the world's meat. An increased use of fertilizers—guano, potash, and nitrates—doubled crop yields while bringing life to previously barren lands. And a safe supply of milk for growing children was ensured by the practice of pasteurization, in which microorganisms were destroyed by high temperatures.

The problem of fresh produce decaying before it reached its market was solved by the development of canning—which involved heat-treating food and then sealing it in airtight metal containers—and refrigeration. Foodstuffs could now be freighted by rail from remote farms in Australia and South America to coastal towns, and then shipped across the world to Europe.

In 1900, the populations of urban areas were still climbing, and the new worldwide food industries were to present political and ecological problems of their own. But the combined efforts of nineteenth-century farmers, entrepreneurs, and scientists had shown that, with careful planning, it would be possible to meet such challenges.

Drawn by a team of thirty-two horses across Oregon's plateau, a threshing machine cuts the standing wheat, ejects the straw, and then deposits the grain in sacks. Mechanized agriculture on farms covering thousands of acres on the plains of North America, Russia, and Eastern Europe dramatically increased the production of cereal crops. In the United States, 2.7 billion bushels of wheat were being harvested annually by 1900; the grain was stored in giant silos at railway depots, and from there it was rushed to major cities. Chicago, a marshy village housing a few score settlers in 1830, had become by the end of the century the largest grain and meat market in the world, with a population of more than one million people.

Cattle destined for slaughter cram the stockyards of Kansas City, Missouri, in the 1880s. Wild long-horned cattle, descendants of the animals that Christopher Columbus shipped from the Canary Islands to Hispaniola in 1493, had roamed across the southern regions of the United States since the sixteenth century; when it was found they could survive cold winters, ranchers drove them north, and by the 1880s, some 45 million head were grazing the plains east of the Rocky Mountains. Toward the end of the decade, their numbers were severely reduced by drought and overgrazing, but on the pampas of South America they continued to multiply. By 1900, the economies of Argentina and Paraguay depended almost entirely on meat exports.

Stacked almost to shoulder height, cans of salmon await distribution from a factory in British Columbia in Canada. Although the contents tasted, according to one consumer, "rather of oil than of fish, with a palpable touch of tin," the processes of canning and refrigeration prevented waste and greatly boosted exports from the Americas and Australia to Europe. Before the 1860s, three-fifths of the cattle carcasses in Argentina rotted before they could be used as meat; in the 1870s, canned mutton from Australia and corned beef from Argentina sold in Britain at less than half the price of locally produced fresh meat. The first refrigerator ship left Argentina for France in 1877, and three years later, the first frozen beef and mutton was shipped from Australia to England.

Exotic fruits and vegetables, fresh dairy products, and a range of canned and bottled goods—as well as an offbeat product labeled "ice-cream powder"—crowd the counters and shelves of a grocery store in turn-of-the-century Chicago. City dwellers in the Americas and Europe were now able to taste foods that their parents had never known or been able to afford. Responding to the influx of new foodstuffs, retailers opened chains of grocery stores that carried either a cornucopia of goods for the wealthy—as shown here—or a more limited range of items that could be purchased cheaply in bulk. And cookbook writers such as Fannie Farmer in the United States and Isabella Beeton in England taught housewives how to use the adjustable heat of their new gas stoves to make sautés, sauces, and soufflés.

THE SCRAMBLE FOR AFRICA

On May 25, 1856, an emaciated, middle-aged Scotsman was borne by African porters into the small town of Quelimane in Portuguese Mozambique. Burning with rheumatic fever, weakened by months of chronic dysentery and recurrent attacks of malaria, he knelt in prayer to thank God for his deliverance at the end of a monumental journey. After traveling for twenty months by foot, ox, donkey, and canoe, David Livingstone, missionary-explorer extraordinary, had become the first European to cross the African continent from coast to coast.

His epic journey of nearly 2,500 miles had begun at the Atlantic port of Luanda in Portuguese Angola and had ended just north of the Zambezi River's broad exit into the Indian Ocean. Along the way, he had repelled an assault by armed warriors, put down a mutiny by his porters, and been partially blinded in one eye. He had encountered evidence of a thriving slave trade that was operated chiefly by Arab merchants, who brought large numbers of Africans out of the interior to be sold to Muslim rulers in the north and across the Indian Ocean. And all the while, in covering mostly uncharted hinterland, he had detailed his geographical discoveries, including that of one of the great scenic wonders of the world: the mighty cataract Africans called the "smoke that thunders," which Livingstone named Victoria Falls in honor of the British sovereign.

In Britain, where Livingstone returned in December to find himself lauded as a national hero, his firsthand accounts of his travels in Africa overturned popular conceptions of the continent. As the *London Journal* commented in December 1856, "Europe had always heard that the central regions of southern Africa were burning solitudes, bleak and barren, heated by poisonous winds, infested by snakes, and only roamed over by a few scattered tribes of untamable barbarians. . . . But Livingstone found himself in a high country, full of fruit trees, abounding in shade, watered by a perfect network of rivers." Even more novel was the emphasis Livingstone himself placed on the commercial as well as the spiritual challenge of Africa. Delivered to packed audiences in lecture halls throughout Britain, his gospel message was distinctly worldly: Missionary work in Africa could succeed only if it marched hand in hand with commercial enterprise. Together, he argued, Christianity and commerce produced civilization.

Livingstone had first arrived in Africa in 1841, when he was posted to a mission station on the northern frontier of Britain's Cape Colony. Within months, he had become convinced that there was more important work to be done than the conversion of the local population and had begun to plan expeditions into regions of Africa never visited by Europeans. Medical studies had played a large part in his missionary training, and he saw it as his duty to bring to the peoples of Africa not just the Christian religion, but the material benefits of medicine and modern science. In

Carved figurines from western Nigeria represent a Yoruba artist's impression of a Catholic priest arriving in his kingdom. During the second half of the nineteenth century, such missionaries did much to spread Christianity in Africa. But they also acted as unconscious harbingers of a less selfless creed. For behind them came European mining prospectors, merchants, and soldiers whose mission—innocently described by Britain's Queen Victoria as "to protect the poor natives and advance civilization"—was to plunder the continent for their own economic benefit.

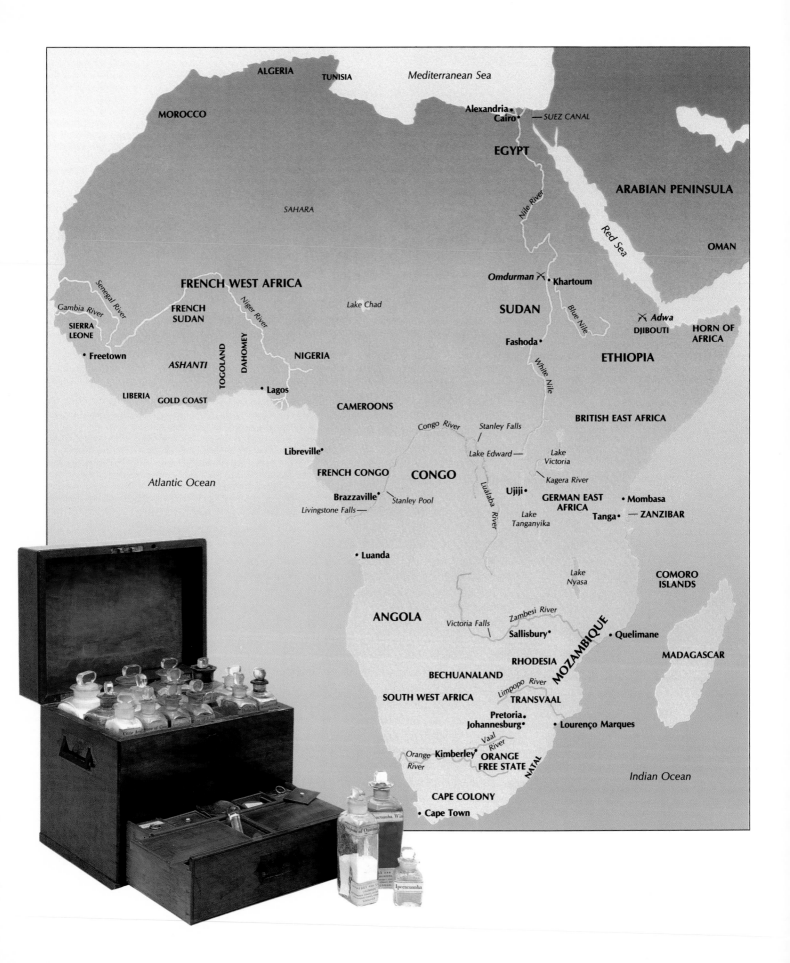

many ways his opinions were too advanced to appeal to the politicians who decided Britain's official state policies; but on a popular level his message commanded a massive response that spread far beyond British shores and contributed to the paternalist moral climate in which colonialism took root.

Britain had unilaterally abolished the transatlantic trade in African slaves in 1807 and had freed the slaves in its colonies in 1833. Missionary societies, appalled by the brutalities of the continuing slave trade in Africa that Livingstone had exposed, now sponsored expeditions to bring the light of civilization into what was popularly known as the dark continent. Ambitious merchants set out to take advantage of new trading opportunities. Adventurers fled the restrictive social conventions of Western society to embrace the unknown.

Without the support of governments, the formal colonization of Africa was slow to follow. But once the pace had been set by private enterprise, the politicians were forced to play their hands, and European intervention in Africa gathered momentum. In the final two decades of the century, the scramble for African territory and wealth came to resemble an exclusively European poker game in which no player dared leave the table for fear that another might walk off with the pot.

By 1900, more than nine-tenths of the continent's 18 million square miles were divided among the European powers into colonies and spheres of influence. In terms of territory, France and Britain were the chief imperial landlords, followed by Germany, Belgium, and Italy. Only Ethiopia in the east and Liberia in the west remained independent of European control. "A sun of disaster has risen in the West," wrote an African poet. "The Christian calamity has come upon us like a dust cloud."

At the time of Livingstone's epic journey in midcentury, only two areas of Africa had been subjected to European colonization on a significant scale: Algeria, which had been invaded by the French in 1830, and the region of present-day South Africa, where Great Britain had seized the Cape from Dutch settlers in 1806 in order to secure the sea route to her developing empire in the East. In Algeria there were some 170,000 white settlers, the majority of Spanish, Italian, or Maltese origin. Roughly the same number of whites lived at the opposite end of the continent, most of them impoverished farmers with little prospect of becoming wealthy. Otherwise, the only white populations of noteworthy number were some 3,000 Portuguese living in Angola and Mozambique.

The west coast of Africa was punctuated by numerous European trading settlements, predominantly British and French, but these were home to only small numbers of white colonists. Most had been founded during the heyday of the transatlantic trade in African slaves in the eighteenth century; more recently the merchants had turned to the export of palm oil, vegetable oils, and timber. There were also three colonies in which most of the settlers were liberated black slaves: at Freetown in Sierra Leone, which became a British colony in 1801; at Libreville in the Gabon estuary, established by the French in 1849; and the independent republic of Liberia, which had been founded in 1821 by an American charity.

Britain's powerful navy was dominant offshore, but its bases in West Africa were intended chiefly to combat the continuing but diminished trade in African slaves and to safeguard commercial enterprises. All the European settlements were coastal enclaves, and the only western region where a foreign power had sought to expand inland was Senegal, where the French had undertaken the systematic conquest of the

Until the mid-nineteenth century, much of Africa—a landmass three times the size of Europe—was protected from most outsiders by the natural barriers of climate, terrain, and the threat of disease. Gradually, technological and medical advances enabled Europeans to prevail over these obstacles: For example, the 1860s medicine chest shown at far left contained quinine, which greatly reduced the death rate from malaria. Following in the wake of explorers and missionaries, traders and settlers competed for what they perceived to be the most commercially profitable territories. By the end of the century, more than 90 percent of the continent had been claimed by the imperial powers of Europe.

An 1878 engraving depicts David Livingstone astride Sinbad, a temperamental ox that accompanied him on one of his epic journeys. Although he once claimed "I sit on my ox and think," the Scottish missionary's forays into Africa involved more than mere meditation. Laboriously using lunar readings to pinpoint his position, Livingstone traveled some 30,000 miles across the continent, enduring rheumatic fever, malaria, and dysentery in his efforts to map its uncharted interior and spread the Christian faith. By the time of his death—probably from ruptured hemorrhoids—in 1873, the published accounts of his travels had made him one of the most famous men in the Western world.

Senegal River basin and pressured the inhabitants to cultivate export crops.

In East Africa, Arab involvement with the indigenous peoples had long preceded any European encroachment. The influence of Islam, the dominant religion along the entire coast by around AD 1000, had led to the development of an Afro-Arab culture known as Swahili. The Swahili coastal entrepôts, through which gold, ivory, and slaves from the interior were channeled to traders from across the Indian Ocean, had come under Portuguese control in the early sixteenth century, but the new colonists failed to make inland progress beyond the lower Zambezi region, where they established a tenuous hold on the province of Mozambique.

In the mid-seventeenth century, the Swahili had made a desperate bid to oust the Portuguese by turning for military assistance to the state of Oman in southern Arabia. The alliance, however, only served to make them subject to even more demanding masters. By the 1820s, the Omani Arabs had seized command of most of the Swahili seaboard, from present-day northern Kenya to southern Tanzania. Their arrival heralded a massive increase in the Indian Ocean slave trade—an upsurge that became even more dramatic after 1832, when the all-powerful sultan of Oman, Sayyid Said, transferred his capital from the scorching climate of Mosquat to the balmier one of Zanzibar.

During the reign of Sayyid Said, as many as 100,000 East Africans were sold into overseas enslavement every year, while many thousands of others were put to work on Zanzibari clove plantations. Consequently, antislavery squadrons, mainly British, became increasingly active along the east coast. Following the death of Sayyid Said in 1856, Zanzibar was brought under British suzerainty.

At this stage, very few Europeans had succeeded in penetrating the African interior. Their progress had been obstructed by the inhospitable terrain and the oppressive climate of the equatorial regions, and more especially by endemic diseases such as malaria and yellow fever, which killed many nonimmune newcomers—missionaries, explorers, and traders alike. But these were not decisive deterrents: European colonizers had overcome difficulties no less formidable in other parts of the world, notably in Central America. Above all, it was the strength of indigenous African societies, especially in the west, that kept white settlers penned up in coastal enclaves. Contrary to popular European belief, central Africa was populated not by undisciplined savages but by well-organized peoples who had the political and military capacity to resist foreign intervention.

On the West African coast the presence and profitability of the European settlements depended on their maintaining the goodwill of African rulers, who demanded what amounted to tax and trading preferences in return for their favor. Even during the eighteenth-century excesses of the slave trade, the West African peoples had retained control of the internal dynamics of commerce, ensuring that the Europeans remained on the coast to await delivery of captives. The Africans had acquired firearms from the Europeans in exchange for slaves, and when the trade dwindled to small-scale illegal traffic they were still able to exploit their diversity of natural resources without becoming tied to European economies. In the mid-nineteenth century, French advances up the Senegal River were checked by the troops of the Muslim reformer al-Hajj Umar. North and northeast of the British presence on the Gold Coast loomed the powerful states of Dahomey and the Ashanti, which numbered their citizens in millions.

On the opposite side of the continent, apart from a few Portuguese traders, only two Europeans—both Mombasa-based German missionaries—had ventured far into the hinterland. In 1848, Johannes Rebmann had reached snow-capped Mount Kilimanjaro, and a year later, Johann Ludwig Krapf had discovered Mount Kenya, similarly crowned in white. In faraway London, both men were branded as liars or hoaxers: Snow, argued the members of the Royal Geographical Society, was a physical impossibility so close to the equator.

Balked in West and East Africa, the European nations were nonetheless becoming increasingly involved in the affairs of the Islamic nations of the north—and they were doing so in a way that did not, at this stage, involve a military or commercial presence. Morocco, an independent sultanate on Algeria's western flank, fell deeply in debt to British financial establishments after borrowing to pay off Spanish invaders in 1859. On Algeria's eastern side, Tunisia, nominally a province of the Ottoman Empire, was incurring huge foreign liabilities that would lead in the 1860s to a commission composed of French, Italian, and British bankers becoming responsible for the country's finances.

Most significant of all was the European economic penetration of Egypt. The process had been snowballing since the accession in 1805 of Muhammad Ali, who set out to create a powerful nation independent of the Ottomans in Istanbul, who had been the country's masters since the sixteenth century. He modernized his army with the aid of French officers, and he used French engineers to build a network of canals and irrigation dams. In 1822, he was persuaded by a French agricultural expert to begin planting cotton, an export crop that linked Egypt to the booming economy of Europe. Under Muhammad Ali's successors in the 1850s, the British built the first railroad in Africa, from Cairo to Alexandria, and Ferdinand de Lesseps, a former French consul, was granted a concession to build a canal linking Port Said on the Mediterranean with Suez on the Red Sea.

With the opening of the Suez Canal in 1869, Egypt became more closely tied to Europe than it had ever been before. Cairo's westernized districts were populated by Europeans who arrived in tens of thousands to settle and open businesses. A burgeoning tourist industry was boosted by the enterprise of Thomas Cook, an Englishman who introduced luxury steamers to take Europeans up the Nile to visit the ancient Egyptian temples at Luxor. Khedive Ismail, Muhammad Ali's grandson, who succeeded in 1863, proudly declared that "My country is no longer in Africa; we are now part of Europe."

All the while, Egypt was moving inexorably toward loss of economic independence. Cotton revenues rose fourfold during the early 1860s, when the United States, previously the world's chief supplier, was torn apart by civil war; but as America recovered toward the end of the decade, the cotton market collapsed. To finance his development programs, Ismail had raised huge loans from European banks, which he now could not repay. In 1875, Britain bought Ismail's half of the shares in the Suez Canal; the other half were owned by France. In the following year, the khedive was forced by his creditors to accept British and French control of the nation's ailing finances.

Even now, the interest of European governments in Africa was limited to the preservation of existing commercial avenues. They remained convinced that the continent's great sub-Saharan interior was too inaccessible, too hazardous, and too hostile to merit colonial expansion. But while the politicians held back, private individuals and companies were responding ever more actively to the mysteries and challenges of the African heartlands.

Before going into exile, the Algerian patriot Abdelkader surrenders his scimitar to the French governor general, the duke of Aumale. The French seized the port of Algiers in 1830, after its governor had hit their consul in the face with a fly swatter. When they tried to colonize the rest of the country, however, Abdelkader rallied the Muslim hill tribes in a holy war and led constant attacks against foreign settlements. Even after his capture and exile in 1847, continued resistance forced settlers to live behind a network of forts garrisoned with France's newly formed foreign legion. Algeria eventually became a French *département*, part of the mother country, in 1871; but it was another eight years before military rule was replaced by civil administration.

For more than a century, missionaries and explorers—mainly British, French, and German—had focused their attention primarily on the four great river systems of the Nile, the Niger, the Zambezi, and the Congo, which seemed to offer the best means of penetrating the interior of the continent. In the 1850s, an obsession developed among British explorers to discover the solution to one of the last great mysteries of geography: the source of the Nile. The origin of the Blue Nile—the river's northern arm, which rises 6,000 feet up in the highlands of Ethiopia—had been settled in 1770 by James Bruce, a Scottish aristocrat-explorer. The search for the source of its much longer arm—the White Nile—began in earnest in 1857, when Britain's Royal Geographical Society sponsored an expedition led by Richard Francis Burton, a thirty-five-year-old army officer who possessed a towering intellect and insatiable curiosity.

Accompanied by another army officer, John Hanning Speke, Burton set out from Zanzibar with 130 porters, crossed the center of present-day Tanzania, and became the first European to set eyes on the vast expanse of Lake Tanganyika. Subsequently, while Burton lay sick with fever, Speke struck out northward and located a second, even larger, lake. He named it after Queen Victoria and concluded that this was the "fountainhead of the Nile."

Speke's claim was fiercely challenged by Burton, who favored Lake Tanganyika as the true source. In 1860, Speke led a second expedition, making a three-year journey from Zanzibar to Lake Victoria, and then down the twisting length of the Nile. From Cairo he cabled home: "The Nile is settled." But Speke had failed to circumnavigate

Victoria, the largest lake in Africa, and establish beyond question that no rivers flowed into it. His dispute with Burton continued to rage.

In September 1864, on the eve of a public debate with Burton, Speke died while shooting birds in the English countryside. There were suggestions that he had committed suicide rather than have his claim demolished and ridiculed for its unscientific basis, but the death was officially judged a hunting accident.

The Royal Geographical Society now persuaded Livingstone, the most celebrated and respected explorer of the age, to take up the search for the Nile's source. After no word was heard from Livingstone for three years, a young reporter on the New York *Herald,* Henry Morton Stanley, was dispatched to find the missing hero. Stanley got his story: In November 1871, he tracked down his quarry at Ujiji, an Arab slaving station on the eastern shore of Lake Tanganyika. But Livingstone, although desperately ill, a self-styled "rackle of bones," refused to abandon his quest. He believed that the source of the Nile was perhaps much farther south than either Burton or Speke had supposed and had become convinced that another major river, the Lualaba, southwest of Lake Tanganyika, was really an early section of the Nile. After bidding Stanley farewell, he set out to follow its course.

On May 1, 1873, in a remote village of present-day Zambia, Livingstone's African servants found their master dead, slumped on his knees as if in prayer. Devotedly, they cut out his heart and viscera and buried them beneath a tree. The body itself was eventually returned to England and was interred in Westminster Abbey.

A sacrificial victim tumbles to his waiting executioners in an 1874 print of the West African kingdom of Dahomey (in modern-day Benin). This annual ceremony—designed to awe the populace—was used by the French in 1892 as a pretext for incorporating the nation into their fast-growing West African empire. But the Dahomean soldiers fought so well that it took two years to subjugate the country. In self-justification, the French troops convinced themselves that their opponents were led by German officers.

Livingstone was sixty years old when he died. Thirty of those years he had spent in Africa: He had journeyed some 30,000 miles, mapped the central African river system, traced the Zambezi to its source, reached the headwaters of the Congo, traversed the Kalahari Desert, and made the first major exploration of Lake Nyasa. As a missionary, he had made few conversions to Christianity. But he had relentlessly opposed the practice of slavery, and he eclipsed all other explorers in his deep understanding of the African peoples, whose languages he learned and whose customs he meticulously recorded.

By contrast, Henry Morton Stanley, nearly thirty years younger than Livingstone, felt no personal attachment to Africa. "I detest the land most heartily," he once wrote. Yet he idolized Livingstone and resolved to complete his hero's last mission. Stanley's own travels were to lead directly to the European colonization of central Africa.

In 1874, leading an expedition equipped with a forty-foot-long portable barge for circumnavigating the huge lakes, Stanley settled the mystery of the White Nile at last. He traced its headwater, the Kagera River, from Lake Victoria to a source 8,000 feet

One of the century's major engineering achievements was the construction of the Suez Canal linking the Mediterranean to the Red Sea. The project was the brainchild of Frenchman Ferdinand de Lesseps, who obtained consent from the khedive of Egypt and in 1859 floated a company to raise money. Ten years later, the completed waterway, shown on the left in a contemporary drawing, ran via three major lakes in its 100-mile route across the Suez isthmus. The expense was enormous—the opening ceremony alone (*above*) cost two million pounds—but so were the benefits: The traveling time between Britain and India was now cut from three months to less than three weeks. And the British, who had initially scoffed at the canal, saw its control as essential to their empire's security. In 1875, they were able to purchase a controlling interest from the bankrupt khedive and secure their lifeline to the east.

up in the mountains of southern Burundi, about thirty miles short of Lake Tanganyika. He went on to discover Lake Edward, due west of Lake Victoria. Then, in November 1876, he set off with some 700 helpers from Nyangwe, west of Lake Tanganyika, to follow the uncharted Lualaba northward. On this river journey, Stanley was twice forced to make major detours overland—first by seven roaring cataracts later known as Stanley Falls, and then, after the river had widened into Stanley Pool, by thirty-two more cataracts, which he named Livingstone Falls. He came under attack by warrior groups and lost hundreds of men by way of desertion and of death from disease and starvation. But he established on this journey that the Lualaba had no connection with the Nile and was, in fact, a part of the Congo, a river more than 3,000 miles long, originating just south of Lake Tanganyika.

In three years, Stanley had surpassed all previous explorers in his efforts to fill in vast blanks on the map of Africa. He had also scored a notable diplomatic success. While visiting the kingdom of Buganda at the northern end of Lake Victoria, he had persuaded its ruler to allow a permanent Christian mission to be established in his country. As a result, both Anglican and Catholic missionaries arrived in 1876. The Anglican mission marked the beginning of a permanent British presence in the East African interior, and this was to lead indirectly to the establishment of the British protectorate of Uganda.

Stanley's ambition was to "put the civilization of Europe into the barbarism of Africa," primarily by way of the Congo. If the British government would organize the construction of a road or railway to bypass the cataracts between Stanley Pool and the river's estuary, he suggested, "the grand highway of commerce to west central Africa" would then be open to them. But his arguments fell on deaf ears, and he found only one European ruler who was prepared to take his ideas seriously.

Belgium, which had separated from the Netherlands to become an independent kingdom in 1831, was one of the smallest of the European nations. But King Leopold II, who had succeeded to the throne in 1865, had never resigned himself to the role of a minor monarch. He had already proposed grandiose schemes for Belgian colonies as far away as China, and now his gaze fell upon the Congo River basin of central Africa. Undeterred by his government's opposition, in September 1876, Leopold sponsored an international conference in Brussels, where he set up an association to promote humanitarian and scientific activities in Africa. As president of this association, Leopold was now free to engage in activities in Africa without the approval of the Belgian government, and without immediately arousing suspicion among other European powers.

In August 1879, Stanley was back in Africa, with money from King Leopold to build a road around Livingstone Falls on the Congo. He also set up trading stations along the 1,000-mile-long route from the mouth of the Congo to Stanley Falls and began to negotiate some 400 treaties with local chiefs for the purpose of creating in the river basin a Confederation of Free Negro Republics. Ostensibly, the confederation was to be an independent black African state; in fact, Stanley was laying the foundation of Leopold's private kingdom of the Congo.

By this time the Congo had excited the attention of other ambitious Europeans. While Stanley was building the road around

French explorer Count Pierre Savorgnan de Brazza cuts a romantic figure in this studio portrait. The Italian-born count was an ardent francophile who considered the continent of Africa to be ideally suited for the expansion of French culture. Photographs such as this one were sold to help finance exploratory expeditions that, during the decade of the 1880s, took de Brazza across immense areas in the regions that lay to the north of the Congo River.

Livingstone Falls, an expedition led by Count Pierre Savorgnan de Brazza, a twenty-six-year-old Italian-born French naval officer, had reached Stanley Pool farther up the river. There, without government authorization, he persuaded a local chief to put his mark on an agreement allowing a French base to be established at his village, the site of present-day Brazzaville. The chief further agreed to place his lands and people under French protection. The French government was at first reluctant to stake an official claim to this territory, but in 1882, political developments in Egypt compelled it to change its mind.

In Egypt, liberal politicians and army officers had formed a militant nationalist movement that sought to rid the country of all foreign influence. The nationalist leader, Colonel Ahmed Arabi, commanded such powerful support that the khedive was compelled to accept him as war minister in a newly formed government. Britain and France, Egypt's principal creditors, suspected that the nationalists might repudiate their country's debts and seize control of the Suez Canal; they also feared for the safety of European lives and property in the area. Therefore, in May of 1882, they jointly sent warships to Alexandria, officially to evacuate refugees but primarily to make a show of strength and deter outbreaks of violence. The Anglo-French naval presence had only a provocative effect. On June 11, about fifty Europeans were killed during a riot in Alexandria.

Britain and France now resolved on a military campaign to safeguard their Egyptian interests, but at the eleventh hour, a domestic crisis prompted the French to withdraw. Britain therefore acted alone, and in August, its expeditionary force routed Ahmed Arabi's troops at Tall al-Kebir, fifty miles northeast of Cairo.

The British occupation that followed was intended only to protect European financial interests and guard the Suez Canal until a responsible Egyptian regime was reestablished. However, it soon became clear that a swift withdrawal was impossible without abandoning Egypt to the defeated nationalists. Moreover, while coping with enormous administrative and economic problems, the British had inherited an additional burden: responsibility for Egypt's defense in the face of the menacing rise of Muhammad Ahmed ibn as-Seyyid Abd Allāh, a Sudanese Muslim who had proclaimed himself the long-expected Mahdi, the "Guided One of the Prophet," with a divine mission to restore the purity of the true faith to the Islamic community.

Seven years were to pass before Egypt was restored to solvency, and an additional nine before the British finally destroyed the belligerent Mahdist state in the Sudan. By then, shifts in the European and Mediterranean power balance had long since given Egypt a strategic importance so great that Britain could not contemplate

In a portrait painted by his wife, the Welsh-born American journalist Henry Morton Stanley wears the uniform of the Congo Free State, which he established on behalf of King Leopold II of Belgium. One of the great adventurers of his age, Stanley resolved many of Africa's geographical mysteries and directly alerted European governments to the continent's commercial potential. His endeavors—which earned him the African name of *Bula Matari,* "the breaker of rocks"—brought him fame, fortune, and in 1899, a British knighthood. Such was Stanley's popular acclaim in the West that his final journey, an expedition in 1887 to rescue Sudan's Egyptian governor from Muslim rebels, was later immortalized in a children's board game *(below).*

withdrawal. Thus, the "temporary" British occupation of 1882 was destined to continue for more than seventy years, in an unwritten system that came to be known as "the veiled protectorate."

Although these developments could not have been foreseen in 1882, the conflict in Egypt shattered the balance of British and French power in Africa, and triggered a new phase in the involvement of European powers. France, jealous of the British occupation of Egypt, now determined to advance its empire in West Africa. In November 1882, the French government agreed to ratify treaties made by Brazza and to sponsor him on a new Congo expedition. In turn, this activity prompted the Portuguese to recall suddenly that they had ventured into the Congo in the late fifteenth century and therefore had a prior claim to the river's estuary. Britain sought to prevent French dominance in the Congo by negotiating an Anglo-Portuguese treaty under which Britain would recognize Portuguese sovereignty over the entire river,

and Portugal, in return, would guarantee Britain access for free trade. And in 1883, the whole escalating competition for dominance in Africa was further complicated by the unexpected intervention of Germany.

Between late 1883 and early 1885, Germany declared protectorates over ill-defined areas in South West Africa, Togoland, the Cameroons, and East Africa. Once again, official government involvement was preceded by the machinations of unauthorized individuals. On a visit to the Cameroons, ostensibly for scientific and commercial purposes, a German explorer named Gustav Nachtigal had made treaties with local chiefs by which they surrendered their lands. Dr. Carl Peters, a German physician, had formed the private Society for German Colonization, and had subsequently negotiated treaties with chiefs in the region of present-day mainland Tanzania. The German chancellor, Otto von Bismarck, had no grand design for an African empire, but he agreed to formalize the German claims under pressure from political factions at home—and because he saw the colonies as a means of deflecting French hostility within Europe, where France was still seething over the loss of Alsace and Lorraine to Germany in 1871.

Having stumbled into Africa without coherent strategies, and having become enmeshed in escalating rivalries, the European powers now recognized a pressing need to sort out their differences. In November 1884, at Bismarck's suggestion, a fourteen-nation conference was convened in Berlin. Its primary purpose was to resolve the question of the Congo's future. Its practical achievement was to lay down the ground rules for an even more rapid and extensive scramble for African territories.

The resolutions approved at the Berlin Congress were designed to slow the pace of colonization and reduce the risk of confrontation among the European powers. Much of central Africa was declared a free-trade zone, thereby dashing the hopes of those who sought to secure protected markets. The decision to make all claims to coastal lands dependent on "effective occupation," which in practice entailed the establishment of an administrative base, increased the costs of running a colony. But at the same time it was agreed that all nations possessing coastal territories had the right to control the hinterland and to expand their borders at will, so long as they did not harm the interests of a neighboring colony. The European presence in Africa was ratified, and the carving up of the continent began in earnest.

Chief among those who gained immediate benefits from the Berlin Congress was Leopold II. Although the conference confirmed French and Portuguese sovereignty over parts of the Congo River basin, some 965,300 square miles of territory stretching deep into the interior were recognized as the Congo Free State, with Leopold's association bearing responsibility for its administration. Leopold ruled this colony not as king of the Belgians but as a private individual, and insisted that "my rights over the Congo are to be shared

A machine gun stands as a lethal symbol of colonial expansion. In 1884, an American-born engineer, Hiram Maxim, developed this light, single-barreled weapon that used the gas pressure created by each shot to operate its automatic loading mechanism. With a range of almost 2,500 yards and a firing capacity of eleven rounds a second, the Maxim shredded African armies: In an 1899 encounter, 320 French troops armed with such weapons were able to rout a Chad force of 12,000.

Carved wooden doors from a palace in southwestern Nigeria show a Yoruba king receiving a British commissioner in 1895. The artistically prolific Yorubas dominated one of three nations that in 1900 were grouped together by British administrators as the protectorate of Nigeria. The resulting territory—larger than any country in western Europe, with 200 spoken languages—consolidated Britain's position in largely French-dominated West Africa.

with none." He amassed a huge fortune from the exploitation of the region's wild rubber, and he maintained a tyrannical reign of terror through his governor general and a locally recruited gendarmerie. Disregarding the conditions agreed at Berlin, he established trading monopolies and introduced a system of forced labor. Torture and mutilation became commonplace; thousands of Africans were to die in the service of a ruler who never even visited their continent.

Treaty diplomacy was the most common means employed by other European nations to impress their power upon Africa. British troops, supported by a much larger force of African allies, had waged war against the Ashanti to the north of the Gold Coast in 1874, and the French became engaged in drawn-out wars against Muslim empires in the western Sudan as they advanced eastward from Senegal; but for both commercial and strategic reasons, peaceful annexation was preferred. Meeting in the conference rooms of Europe, diplomats drew lines across inaccurate maps of the African continent rather than risk a confrontation between their military forces. Within Africa itself, treaties with local rulers enabled trading-company agents to stake out massive protectorates, which could then be administered by a handful of government officials.

A picture executed by an East African artist depicts the slaughter as ill-armed warriors clash with fully equipped Swahili *Schutztruppen*—black troops led by European officers—in the German protectorate of Tanganyika. Occupation of the territory, which was initially run, like most other German possessions, by a commercial company, met with stiff opposition. Not until the end of the century was even minimal government established.

In West Africa, the region that offered the greatest potential profits to European traders, the British government sought to counter French expansion along the Niger River and to increase its own influence as cheaply as it could by giving support to the Royal Niger Company, a chartered association of merchants. Agents of the company who negotiated with African chiefs were equipped with standard printed forms, to be filled in after an interpreter had explained their meaning to the Africans. The first paragraph of one such blank treaty read: "We, the undersigned chiefs of . . . , with the view to the betterment of the condition of our country and people, do this day cede to the Royal Niger Company (Chartered and Limited), for ever, the whole of our territory extending from. . . ."

In East Africa a boundary commission set up by Germany, Britain, and France in 1886 allocated to Germany the area later to become known as Tanganyika, while recognizing the roughly defined regions of modern Kenya and Uganda as spheres of British influence. French interests were limited to the Comoro Islands, Madagascar, and a stronghold on the Horn of Africa at Djibouti.

The eastern interior of the continent offered no economic rewards without the risk of massive investment for the development of agriculture. In the late 1880s, however, a new consideration compelled the British government to take an active interest in this area. The nation that controlled the headwaters of the Nile in Uganda might have the power to divert the flow of British Egypt's lifeblood, and when the German entrepreneur Carl Peters began signing treaties with African chiefs in the vicinity of Lake Victoria, a clash between the imperialist powers of Europe appeared to be imminent.

But diplomacy prevailed. By the terms of the Heligoland Treaty of 1890, Germany recognized British claims to Uganda, and Great Britain acknowledged the German presence below a line starting south of Mombasa and drawn directly northwest to Lake Victoria—the present-day Kenya-Tanzania boundary. Uganda was formally proclaimed a British protectorate in 1894, and in the following year, the British government agreed to finance the construction of a railroad between Mombasa and Lake Victoria.

In December 1895, the last great engineering enterprise of the Victorian era was begun. The construction of the Uganda Railway entailed importing more than 30,000 workers from India and laying nearly 600 miles of railroad track over unmapped savanna and scrubland. To finance this massive project, agriculture and white settlement were encouraged, primarily in the highlands of present-day Kenya, where the soil was rich and the climate bracing. The same pattern was to follow in German East Africa, where the Central Railway, starting on the coast at Tanga, slowly advanced into the interior.

So far, the European powers had contrived to partition the greater part of Africa without once becoming involved in military conflict among themselves. Open hostilities had been avoided by complex diplomatic alignments: The Portuguese presence in Angola and Mozambique, for example, was supported by France and Germany as a means of preventing British expansion in southern Africa. But in the 1890s, a number of factors combined to sharpen European competition, and the safety net of peaceful diplomacy threatened to give way.

As the number of white settlers increased, the efforts of colonial administrations became focused on controlling the supply of African labor. At the same time, the widespread purchase of European firearms by African peoples in the western Sudan and along the eastern coast of the continent led to increased conflict both among rival African states and between Africans and their new European overlords. And in the capitals of Europe, there emerged a new breed of stridently imperialist politicians whose ambitions extended beyond the limits of purely commercial or strategic considerations.

In the west and north of Africa, France and Britain had become locked in a lethal game of tick-tack-toe. The former, whose troops had been engaged in the subjugation of Muslim powers to the south of the Sahara since the early 1880s, dreamed of an empire extending from the west to the east of the continent; the latter sought dominion over a single swath of territory from north to south, linking Cairo to the Cape. In a period of escalating violence, a major confrontation between these two dominant European powers in Africa appeared inevitable.

In March 1896, a 17,000-strong Italian army that was attempting to occupy Ethiopia was crushingly defeated by the French-armed troops of the Ethiopian emperor, Menelik. The battle left Italian nationals isolated at their outpost in the eastern Sudan, in grave danger of being attacked by the militant Mahdists. Italy, strongly supported by its German allies, appealed for diversionary help. Great Britain, fearing that the French were about to advance toward the Nile from the west, responded by sending an Anglo-Egyptian army commanded by General Horatio Herbert Kitchener to invade the Sudan.

What began as a token show of strength developed into a major military campaign. Ten years before, after a British garrison at Khartoum under General Charles Gordon had been wiped out by the Mahdists, the British had decided that the reconquest of the Sudan was economically impracticable. But now Egypt was prosperous, and security of the Upper Nile had become Britain's paramount concern in Africa. The farther Kitchener advanced, the stronger was the demand for the complete destruction of the Mahdist state.

The decisive battle was fought in September 1898 outside Omdurman, the town across the Nile from Khartoum where the Mahdi, who had died in 1895, was buried. Kitchener's army, 20,000 strong and armed with Maxim machine guns, routed the Mahdist army, killing some 11,000 warriors and wounding another 16,000. To make his annihilation of the Mahdist state complete, Kitchener destroyed the Mahdi's

Clad in full-dress uniforms, victorious Ethiopian officers pose for a European photographer. Ethiopia had the best indigenous army in the continent and was one of the few African states to avoid colonization. In 1885, the Italians seized Ethiopian territory on the Red Sea to form the colony of Eritrea, and a few years later, they advanced inland. But the emperor of Ethiopia had imported European military advisers and equipped his men with modern weaponry—much of it bought from Italy itself. After several defeats, the Italian army was annihilated, and in 1896, Italy recognized Ethiopia's independence in return for the right to remain in the coastal settlements.

tomb, exhumed the body, and sent the skull to the London College of Surgeons.

In Britain the slaughter was hailed as a heroic triumph. One year after Queen Victoria's diamond jubilee, pride in the British empire was at its zenith; and the Sudan, though conquered in Egypt's name, was popularly regarded as a new British possession. Just one complication remained. Six weeks before Omdurman, Captain Jean-Baptiste Marchand, with six other French officers and 120 Senegalese troops, had completed an epic 3,000-mile march from the French Congo to the banks of the Upper Nile. Some 400 miles south of Khartoum, the tricolor was flying over a village of mud huts named Kodok.

After his victory at Omdurman, Kitchener's orders were to proceed upriver and dislodge any French forces he encountered. And so, at Kodok, his mighty battalions were ranged against Marchand's ludicrously small band of soldiers. The two commanders happened to take an instant liking to each other. Nevertheless, after they had wined and dined together, Marchand remained adamant: Although he conceded that his position was hopeless, he could not withdraw his troops without receiving fresh orders from Paris. If necessary, he would die in defense of the newly claimed French territory.

When news of the encounter reached Europe, the newspapers of both France and Britain were filled with expressions of righteous fury. France insisted that the region had no internationally recognized government and was therefore open to possession by any power that could establish "effective occupation." Britain argued that the Sudan belonged to the Egyptians who, temporarily, had been unable to exercise jurisdiction there.

For two months, fears of a major European war loomed large. But finally the French government, assailed by economic difficulties at home and lacking support in Africa, backed down. Under the terms of the Anglo-French Declaration of March 1899, France was excluded from the entire Nile River valley. Soon afterward, by advancing in three directions—from the French Congo, Algeria, and the upper Ni-

An oil painting of the battle at Omdurman shows desperate British lancers charging through a throng of dervishes—Muslim fundamentalists who had sworn to drive the Egyptians out of the Sudan. During the five-hour battle, on September 2, 1898, an Anglo-Egyptian army led by General Horatio Herbert Kitchener routed their foe with ease: 11,000 dervishes littered the field while just forty of Kitchener's men were killed. The encounter, however, had a bitter coda. When a few hundred dervishes prepared to make a final stand, 320 British lancers charged. Suddenly another 2,000 warriors rose from a hidden ditch directly ahead. Driven by their momentum, the lancers slammed through to safety. But the cost was terrible: In just two minutes, 119 horses and 77 lancers were killed or wounded.

ger—France was to create a vast empire in west and central Africa. But recognition of an Anglo-Egyptian Sudan ended the dream of establishing an all-French route across the continent, and with it an empire that would link the Mediterranean, the Atlantic, and the Indian Ocean.

The land over which France and Great Britain had almost come to war consisted, in the words of the British consul general in Egypt, of "large tracts of useless territory that it would be difficult and costly to administer." Chauvinism had become one of the most compelling factors in the competition among the European powers. But in the final stage of the scramble for the control of Africa, there was one quarter of the vast continent where economic motives remained a dominant force; and here, for the first time, the struggle for profit as well as prestige would set whites against whites in open warfare.

In midcentury, the temperate south of Africa was divided between the British

colonies of the Cape and Natal, the Boer republics of Orange Free State and the Transvaal, and a number of independent African states. The Boer—meaning "farmer" in Dutch—colonists were descendants of Dutch settlers who had come to the Cape in the late seventeenth and the eighteenth centuries and of Protestant refugees from other European countries who had joined them. The British, whose presence on the Cape was sufficient to maintain the security of their sea route to India, had no desire to expand their dominions. But the discovery of mineral wealth was to release keen imperialist ambitions.

The first known diamond to be discovered in southern Africa was found in 1866 by a fifteen-year-old boy strolling along a bank of the Orange River in the far north of Cape Colony. Soon, new finds were reported along the Orange and Vaal rivers, and on the farmland of two Boer brothers named de Beer. This region, known as Kimberley, was to become the greatest diamond-producing region in the world.

All the major diamond discoveries were on territory inhabited by the Griqua, a people of mixed Afro-European stock, specifically Boer pioneers and Khoikhoi cattle herders. Their land rights were now fiercely challenged by the Boers of the Orange Free State and the Transvaal and by newly arrived fortune hunters who had proclaimed their own independent republic in the region. But it was the British who, in 1873, annexed the diamond-rich territory now known as Griqualand West.

Four years later, Britain's colonial secretary, Lord Carnarvon, proclaimed the annexation of the Transvaal. His primary purpose was to advance his dream of creating a British-dominated confederation of states in southern Africa, as had been achieved in Canada. The Boers lacked the economic and military strength to resist the British drive, but a number of African states began to take up arms.

Unashamedly admiring, a cartoon of Britain's greatest empire builder, Cecil Rhodes, caricatures his dream to see British possessions running from the Cape to Cairo. Traveling between Britain's Oxford University and the diamond mines of Kimberley, Rhodes gained by the age of thirty both a classics degree and one of the world's largest personal fortunes. Although his imperial ambitions were thwarted—his last words were reported to be "So little done, so much to do"—his enormous impact on southern Africa prompted American novelist Mark Twain to comment: "When Rhodes stood upon the Cape Peninsula his shadow fell upon the Zambezi."

Black and white employees of the Republic Gold Mining Company are photographed in 1888, two years after the first major strike on Transvaal's Witwatersrand gold reef. Such early mines required very little capital: just enough to pay for rudimentary tools and a small African labor force. Later, however, as shafts plunged deeper into the Rand, the enterprise demanded costly machinery and massive manpower, which could be financed only by millionaires such as Cecil Rhodes. By 1900, Transvaal had become the world's largest gold producer; but to the chagrin of the Boers, every one of the mine owners was an uitlander, or outsider.

The British attempted to placate the Zulus, the most powerful African people in the region, by offering to return Boer-annexed lands if they would stand down their army. This proposal was rejected. In January 1879, when crossing the Natal border to enforce the demobilization of the Zulu army, a British force suffered an overwhelming defeat at Iswandhlwana. Nearby, at Rorke's Drift, a much smaller British force only narrowly escaped a similar fate when they were beseiged by 4,000 Zulus. It was to be another six months before the British achieved a major victory that led to a peace settlement.

Meanwhile, encouraged by the Zulus' initial success, the Boers of the Transvaal had become increasingly militant, and in December 1880, they launched a war of independence. The only British battalion within the Transvaal was ambushed and defeated, and in February 1881, the Boers routed a force of some 500 British troops at Majuba Hill, near the Natal border. The British government, in a conciliatory mood, agreed that the Transvaalers should be granted internal autonomy, while remaining subject to British suzerainty in their dealings with foreign powers and with African peoples.

The key figure behind the resurgence of Transvaal republicanism was Paul Kruger,

A watercolor shows British cavalry galloping through scattered Zulu corpses to relieve the defenders of the mission station at Rorke's Drift. Britain's annexation of Zulu territory in southern Africa proved a traumatic campaign. When British soldiers marched into Zululand in 1879 to force the warlike Zulus to lay down their arms, they were confronted by a well-organized and disciplined foe. On January 22, one invading column was wiped out at Iswandhlwana; that afternoon, 4,000 warriors attacked the makeshift hospital at Rorke's Drift, where about thirty sick soldiers were defended by a garrison of eighty. For twelve hours of terrible close-quarter combat the besieged men kept their foe at bay, until at dawn the exhausted Zulus departed.

who had been vice president at the time of Britain's annexation of his country. A die-hard traditionalist who was steeped in the fundamentalist teachings of the Calvinist faith, he was also a shrewd politician whose wily diplomacy would make him the most formidable opponent of British imperialism in Africa throughout the last two decades of the century.

Kruger began his seventeen-year presidency of the Transvaal in 1883. At the same time, in Cape Colony, a young Englishman was emerging as a major force in the region's politics. Cecil John Rhodes had first journeyed to southern Africa at the age of seventeen in 1870, after the doctor treating him for tuberculosis had recommended a warm climate and life in the open air. Every young man, Rhodes believed, should resolve his main purpose in life, and his own was to promote the expansion of the British empire: "If there be a God," he once said, "I think what he would like me to do is to paint as much of Africa British red as possible." The full scale of his ambitions was revealed in a will that he wrote in 1877, in which he envisaged a federal empire incorporating the whole continent of Africa, the Holy Land, the valley of the Euphrates, all of South America, the Malay Archipelago, and the seaboards of China and Japan. He also hoped that the United States might be brought back into the fold of the British empire, as an integral part of a federated power so great "as to hereafter render wars impossible."

For all the extravagance of this vision, in the rough-and-tumble frontier world of the Kimberley diamond fields, Rhodes showed himself to be a hardened realist. Recognizing from the outset that wealth was the key to power, he pursued it relentlessly. In partnership with another young Englishman, Charles Rudd, Rhodes cornered the market in steam pumps, which he then rented out to miners whose workings were threatened with flooding. He invested in an ice-making machine that enabled the Kimberley saloons to provide cold drinks. Most important, he and Rudd concentrated on buying out individual claim holders, many of whom had become discouraged or bankrupt as their deeper diggings came up against hard blue rock. In 1880, the two partners formed the De Beers Mining Company, Limited. Subsequently Rhodes was to take over all of his major rivals and win control of 90 percent of the world's diamond output.

Meanwhile, having won election to the Cape parliament in 1881, Rhodes used his prodigious wealth to increase his political influence. He acquired a controlling interest in a group of Cape newspapers and promoted a scare-mongering campaign to persuade the British government to seize control of the Bechuana plains, stretching from the northern borders of Cape Colony to the upper Zambezi valley. The establishment of the Bechuanaland Protectorate in 1885 was designed to prevent further Boer encroachment into African territory; it also reduced the possibility of German and Boer expansion blocking a British advance north from the Cape.

Kruger's republic was now almost completely surrounded by British territory. But then, all at once, the balance of power was dramatically transformed in the Transvaal's favor. In 1886, great gold discoveries were made on the Witwatersrand, a highland region to the south of Pretoria that was popularly known as the Rand. The Transvaal, hitherto the poorest of the European-dominated communities, was about to become the richest. And along with increased economic power, there were renewed hopes for Kruger's dream of creating a united white southern Africa under Boer leadership.

Rhodes reacted swiftly to the challenge. In 1888, by means of a treaty with Lobengula, king of the Matabele, he secured exclusive mining rights in the region north of the Transvaal. The following year, he persuaded the British government to grant his newly formed British South Africa Company a royal charter for the exploitation of the vaguely defined area of "Zambezia," a region that consisted of almost 400,000 square miles embracing Matabeleland and Mashonaland to its northeast. The company's wide powers included the right to make laws and preserve the peace with its own police force.

Lobengula had signed away the mining concession in exchange for a paltry monthly income, 1,000 rifles, and 10,000 rounds of ammunition. At the time, he believed that Rhodes was interested only in seeking gold. But he quickly recognized his error. "Did you ever see a chameleon catch a fly?" he asked a missionary in 1889. "England is the chameleon and I am the fly."

True enough, the British acquisition of mining rights was followed by an armed invasion of the Matabele realm. In June 1890—the year he became premier of Cape Colony—Rhodes sent out a pioneer column comprising nearly 200 white and 150 black settlers, plus some 500 armed police, ostensibly a peacekeeping force for the expected gold rush. In September, at a far northern outpost that they named Salisbury

THE BOER WAR: STRUGGLE FOR THE VELD

The conflict of interest between British ambitions in southern Africa and the fierce independence of the Boer republics led, in 1899, to war. Trained in the formal warfare of Europe, the slow-moving British were baffled by the Boers' guerrilla tactics and frustrated by their foe's ability to supply their forces in the field. After suffering heavy losses and being ignominiously besieged at Kimberley, Ladysmith, and Mafeking, the British army resorted to a war of attrition, burning crops, herding noncombatants into concentration camps, and covering the countryside with a network of fortified blockhouses. By 1902, wealth and force of numbers had prevailed; but it had taken 450,000 troops to subdue an army of fewer than 88,000.

Three generations of Boers bear arms for independence. All Boer men over the age of fourteen were required to fight; and although they had neither uniforms nor training, their faith in the justice of their cause made them a formidable enemy.

A lookout keeps watch above the neat lines of a British camp. No longer dressed in the traditional scarlet tunic that made him an easy target in the African veld, he wears instead the army's newly adopted khaki drab.

after the British prime minister of the day, the pioneers raised the Union Jack and took possession of Mashonaland in the queen's name.

Mashonaland did not turn out to be the region of King Solomon's legendary mines, as had been popularly believed, but Rhodes was undeterred. Aided by Leander Starr Jameson, a Scottish doctor whose personal charm masked a ruthless will, Rhodes was determined to keep alive his dream of an all-British route from the Cape to Cairo. In 1893, after Lobengula's warriors had resumed their traditional raids on the Mashona, Jameson demanded their complete withdrawal from the region. He then launched a full-scale war on the Matebele, who fell by the thousands before the pioneers' cannons and Maxim machine guns. Rhodes had his own colony at last, a country to be named Rhodesia and widely settled by farmers and miners, with the Matabele providing the main work force.

Three years later, the Matabele and the Mashona rose in rebellion, waging warfare on isolated white settlements. Rhodes himself ended the conflict in 1897 when, unarmed and accompanied by only three white companions, he rode into the Matopo Hills to find the rebel leaders and negotiate a peace settlement. It was to be his last notable achievement.

In 1894, the completion of a railroad to Delagoa Bay had freed the Boers of the Transvaal from dependence on the British for an outlet for their trade. Rhodes's main hope of regaining the initiative now rested on attacking the republic from within, by encouraging discontent among the tens of thousands of foreign mineworkers who had flooded into the Transvaal. Kruger was so alarmed by the threat that these uitlanders, or outsiders, posed to the traditional Boer way of life that he raised the voting requirements to fourteen years' residence and a minimum voting age of forty. Thereafter, agitation for increased franchise rights steadily mounted, primarily on the Rand, where nearly 90 percent of some 50,000 whites were uitlanders, and some two-thirds of them were British.

Rhodes was convinced that an uprising by the uitlanders was planned for December 28, 1895. He reasoned that a breakdown of law and order would provide a justifiable cause for British forces to invade the Transvaal, and he prepared an armed force under the leadership of Jameson on the Transvaal border with Bechuanaland. But there was no uprising. Impetuously, Jameson decided to act alone. He rode into the Transvaal at the head of a column of 478 British South Africa Company police, driving toward Johannesburg, where he expected to rally massive support.

Jameson's force was ambushed and captured at Doornkop, forty miles short of Johannesburg. Jameson himself was extradited for trial in England, where he was found guilty of preparing "a military expedition against a friendly state" and sentenced to fifteen months' imprisonment. Rhodes's involvement in the fiasco proved to be his downfall, and he was forced to resign his premiership.

The Jameson Raid, though a petty event in itself, had far-reaching effects. It convinced even the most skeptical Boers that British policy was directed toward the complete overthrow of their republics. Indirectly, it led to a wave of anti-German feeling in Britain, since Emperor William II, sympathizing with the Boers, had sent President Kruger a telegram congratulating him on his successful defense of the Transvaal. And it stiffened the resolve of the British to recoup their losses and impose their own will on Kruger.

In April 1897, Alfred Milner sailed to the Cape as its new high commissioner. He and the British colonial secretary, Joseph Chamberlain, determined to subject Kruger

British tourists, accompanied by porters from Thomas Cook and Son, clamber precariously over Egypt's Great Pyramid in the 1870s. Toward the end of the nineteenth century, Africa became a popular tourist destination for Europe's leisure classes. Many took advantage of tours arranged by operators such as Thomas Cook to marvel at the continent's landscape and inhabitants, while others went on safaris to hunt its diminishing wildlife. Long after the colonial powers had departed, their legacy of tourism would remain.

to more and more demands for internal reforms, and to portray their adversary as an oppressive tyrant. They recognized that only war was now likely to force the Transvaal into a federation under the British flag. But when war came, they wanted to ensure that Kruger was seen as the villain and that British public opinion was on their side.

Under pressure, Kruger made one concession after another, but these were never enough. In June 1898, he despairingly cried "It is our country you want," and he was right. On October 9, 1899, Kruger demanded the withdrawal within forty-eight hours of all British troops massed on the Transvaal's borders. On Chamberlain's instructions, Milner replied that this request was "impossible to discuss." Three days later, the Boers launched simultaneous attacks at Mafeking, Kimberley, and Ladysmith. The most futile of African wars had begun.

The British expected the war to be over by Christmas. Instead it lasted for two and a half years, during which time the Boer militias, fighting for their freedom, repeatedly humbled the regular British troops. During the latter stages of the war, the British, frustrated by Boer guerrilla raids, resorted to extreme measures. More than 150,000 women, children, and African workers from villages that sustained Boer fighters were interned in depots known as concentration camps. Lacking adequate food and sanitation facilities, 26,000 inmates of the camps died.

In May 1902, the Boers, outnumbered by massive reinforcements sent out from Britain, were finally brought to submission. But victory had cost the lives of 6,000 British soldiers killed in action, plus another 16,000 who died of typhoid fever and other diseases. Rhodes, the most passionate of empire builders, had died two months before the war's end and lay buried in the Matopo Hills of his prized Rhodesian colony. Kruger, who had fled to Holland early in the war, died two years later and was buried in his old capital of Pretoria.

In 1910, as the British instigators of the war had always intended, the annexed Boer republics were formally combined with the colonies of Natal and the Cape to create the Union of South Africa. The Africans, large numbers of whom had fought and died on both sides in the war, were given no voice in the all-white convention that decided the future shape of their motherland. Furthermore, by the Natives Land Act of 1913, black South Africans—outnumbering whites by at least four to one—were denied the right to own land on 87 percent of the Union's territory. The remaining 13 percent

Beneath the portraits of Emperor William II and his wife, a Swahili schoolboy leads his class in a writing lesson. European governments were keen to maintain law and order in their colonies; but the education of their new subjects was left almost entirely to missionaries. The subjects taught were rudimentary, and the schools were—unlike this solid construction in Dar es Salaam, the capital of Tanganyika—usually makeshift reed buildings dotted about the bush. Nevertheless, the mission schools emerged as one of the few avenues of advancement open to Africans under colonial rule.

included some of the most marginal farming land and contained no major town or industrial district. The war between British and Boer colonists had given birth to the most aggressive of all the colonial regimes.

The bold slashes of color on the map of Africa that denoted European-controlled territories at the end of the nineteenth century were impressive enough, but they belied the confusion that reigned in the continent itself. Many Europeans themselves were uncertain of what they had achieved. Slavery within Africa had been largely abolished, but what had replaced it fell far short of the noble concept of civilization envisaged by Livingstone in the early years of European penetration. In 1902, the

young Winston Churchill, the future British prime minister, who had led a cavalry charge in the battle at Omdurman in 1898, noted that "the inevitable gap between conquest and dominion becomes filled with the figures of the greedy trader, the inopportune missionary, the ambitious soldier, and the lying speculator, who disquiet the minds of the conquered and excite the sordid appetites of the conquerors. And as the eye of thought rests on these sinister features, it hardly seems possible for us to believe that any fair prospect is approached by so foul a path."

The colonies were essentially a mercantile creation, yet even the traders, reckoning up their profit-and-loss accounts, must have wondered at the expense of so much effort. Except for South Africa, the colonies afforded little economic gain: There was no great demand in Europe for African products, and Africa was of very limited value as an export market.

The scramble for territory had been conducted, as the word suggests, haphazardly, rapaciously, without long-term strategies. It was as if the object had been simply to seize territory, the currency in which imperial might had traditionally been reckoned, and then, in the words of a British administrator on the Gold Coast, "as much as possible to rule the country as if there were no inhabitants."

But of course there were inhabitants. They vastly outnumbered their white overlords; and despite their lack of formal political rights, the continent remained theirs. European culture had been imposed on only limited sectors. The great majority of Africans remained unaffected by the European introduction of hospitals, schools, railroads, and embryo industries, almost all of which were planned to serve the colonists' exclusive interests. And as the European administrators in the early years of the twentieth century sought to make their colonies self-sufficient and their subjects docile taxpayers, the Africans struggled with their own problems and evolved their own solutions. Most of them resisted European attempts to draw them into a wage-earning proletariat and chose instead to live as peasants or migrant workers, retaining control over their own labor and a fair measure of their produce. Even those whose best land had been expropriated proved to be more efficient farmers than the white colonists. To the Europeans, the Africans remained as separate and as ill-comprehended as they had been before the scramble began.

THE PEOPLE'S ART

In 1859, Napoleon III of France delayed the march of his army through the streets of Paris while he entered a photographer's studio to have his picture taken. Fashionable society rushed to follow his example, and the trend soon spread throughout Europe and to America. In London alone, more than 250 portrait studios were doing a healthy business by the mid-1860s.

Many portraits were reproduced as *cartes de visite* on small cards measuring two by four inches, such as those shown above. Their mass production was made possible by the wealth of technical improvements that had followed the first experiments in photography by Louis-Jacques Daguerre in France and W. H. Fox Talbot in England in the 1830s. Among the more significant were the use of a light-sensitive substance known as collodion in the developing process, which reduced exposure times, and a technique that was devised in the 1850s for taking up to ten photographs on a single glass plate.

These innovations made the immortality conferred by portraiture available for the first time to the commonfolk. A London newspaper noted in 1861 that photography had "swept away many of the illiberal distinctions of rank and wealth, so that the poor man who possesses but a few shillings can command as perfect a lifelike portrait of his wife or child as Sir Thomas Lawrence painted for the most distinguished sovereigns of Europe."

Nor were portraits the only benefits that photography brought. As the following pages show, intrepid travelers returned with images of remote lands and peoples for an avid armchair audience; journalists made visible the true drama of wars and other newsworthy events. The experiments of Eadweard Muybridge, who used batteries of cameras to photograph humans and animals in motion, provided artists and scientists with information unable to be discerned by the naked eye.

Toward the end of the century, the democratization of photography was completed with the introduction of lightweight, compact cameras whose use required no special knowledge or skills. Consumers became producers, because those who wanted a visual record of their lives now made it themselves. Next to language, photography had become the most accessible medium of communication and delight.

I stroll through Rhenish vineyards, I sit under Roman arches . . . I pass, in a moment, from the banks of the Charles to the ford of the Jordan." So wrote the American author Oliver Wendell Holmes of his collection of stereographs—pairs of photographs with slightly different perspectives that, when viewed through a stereoscope, appeared to be three-dimensional. To satisfy such vicarious travelers, photographers risked life and limb hauling their packs of equipment across icy glaciers or burning deserts. Their success was never certain: In 1857 in Egypt, the English photographer Francis Frith described how he processed his prints "in a smothering little tent, with my collodion fizzing-boiling up all over the glass." But, against the odds, Frith and other pioneers made available to an excited public the landscapes, art, and social customs of faraway countries they would not otherwise have seen.

This photograph of a street in Canton was reproduced in 1873 in a four-volume pictorial survey of Chinese society by the Scottish photographer John Thomson. Traveling in China for five years, Thomson recorded mundane street scenes and more sensational activities, such as tortures and executions, with an inquisitive eye; he also noted routes and sites that might be of use to European colonizers.

Dating from around 1880, this hand-tinted photograph of the tattooed back of a Japanese man was taken for a Western public that had developed a keen appetite for the exotic.

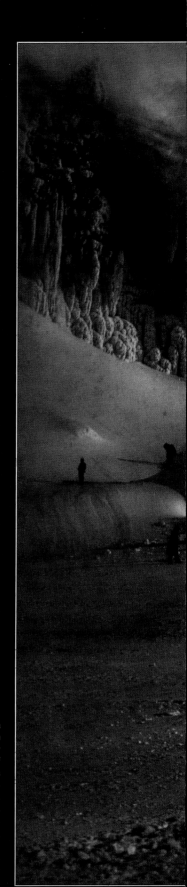

Sightseers cluster on a snowy expanse beneath the wondrous immensity of Niagara Falls, some of whose tumbling waters have been turned into pillars of ice. Taken by H. Nielson in the 1880s, this was one of many photographs that, by awakening the American public to the beauty of their landscapes, contributed to the creation of national parks.

Long before the 1890s, when photographs began to appear in newspapers and magazines, their shock value as eyewitness records was well understood—as was their power to condition the public's response to the events they recorded. In the American Civil War, pictures of the slain taken by Mathew Brady and others undermined the heroic concept of war conveyed by traditional paintings. Photographs of skeletal prisoners of war at Andersonville in Georgia were instrumental in securing the death sentence for the camp commander. In Britain, social reformers such as Dr. Thomas Barnardo used photographs to dramatize the plight of the poor and homeless.

But the camera possessed no intrinsic guarantee of neutrality; and photography could as easily be used to persuade as it could to provide information.

The moment before a rebel feels the blow of his executioner's sword is captured in this photo taken in China around 1900 by Benjamin West Kilburn, an American.

The menace and squalor of a New York slum in 1888 are revealed by the journalist-reformer Jacob Riis, a Danish immigrant. His photographs alerted the public to the desperation of the city's poor.

A French commander in the Crimean War (above) directs the attention of his staff officers. This photograph was taken by Roger Fenton, who arrived in the Crimea in 1855 with two assistants and a converted wine-merchant's wagon (left), which served as his house trailer and dark-room. Fenton pointed his camera well away from the actual horrors of the war, and his photographs were used by British politicians to refute allegations of military incompetence.

The box-shaped, no-frills Kodak camera manufactured by the U.S. inventor George Eastman in 1888 literally placed photography in the hands of an enormous new public. "You press the button, we do the rest" was the accurate advertising slogan: The camera came loaded with a roll of film, and after taking 100 exposures, the owner returned the complete package to the manufacturer for processing and printing. In 1900, Eastman launched a new version, the Brownie, which cost only one dollar. More than 500,000 of these cameras were sold over the next sixteen years.

The first hand-held Kodak was 3¼ by 6⅝ by 3⅞ inches high. The film was advanced by turning a key projecting from the top.

The subjects and themes of the photographs below—a holiday abroad, fooling around in the garden, an outing in a hired rowboat, a pony with its proud owner—typify the everyday scenes that hand-held cameras were tailor-made to celebrate. All these photographs were taken during the first four years of the Kodak camera's manufacture, when a circular mask was fitted to eliminate areas of poor resolution in the corners of each frame.

Unaware that they are being photographed, a rapt audience listens to a beach entertainer, and two over-dressed women get their skirt hems wet at a seaside resort in Norfolk, England. These unposed, spontaneous snaps were taken in 1892 by a young amateur photographer named Paul Martin, who disguised his camera as a leather box.

THE SHAPING OF AUSTRALIA

To immigrants from Britain arriving around the middle of the nineteenth century, certain aspects of Australia appeared reassuringly familiar. They were greeted by voices speaking English, and many found homes in settlements that bore the same names as British places or were named after British politicians or royalty. Churches and town halls were built in the neo-Gothic style and looked indistinguishable from those in Britain. But Australia was more than 14,000 miles from Britain, and the resemblances—though betraying deep bonds between the early settlers and their homeland—were deceptive. Behind the strip of coastal settlements lay the emptiness of the outback, the vast uncharted deserts of the continent's interior. And there was the emptiness too of memory, an absence of the many forms of cultural history—ancient buildings, literature, customs, and traditions—that give a nation its identity.

In 1852, an Australian-born journalist named Daniel Deniehy placed a challenging emphasis on the colonists' predicament. "We have no long line of poets or statesmen or warriors in this country," he wrote, concluding : "It is ours, then, to inaugurate the future." Over the next decades, it was to the task of building a future, of forging their identity as a people and as a nation, that the Australian settlers dedicated themselves.

Although Australia was to remain a part of the British empire, Britain was to play a minor role in this process. In 1788, the first British fleet to arrive in Australia had carried not skilled and determined adventurers but criminals for whom there was no room in the jails: Britain's purpose was to found a penal settlement in a remote region, not to establish a colony. The government granted charters to private companies, encouraged investment in their projects, and approved constitutions for local government, but it was the settlers who took the initiative in colonizing Australia.

They were also blessed with luck: In an earlier age, the colonists would not have possessed the technology to tame their environment so rapidly, nor would their mother country have had the wealth to invest in their ventures. But their achievement was still astounding, a rags-to-riches story on a continental scale. After a grim beginning and only gradual progress during the first sixty years, the pace of development rapidly accelerated from 1850 onward, and by the end of the century, Australians no longer thought of themselves as colonists but as proud citizens of a new-forged nation. The Commonwealth of Australia, formally established in 1901, had probably the highest standard of living in the world and was the most advanced social democracy of its time. It was a country many in Britain had reason to envy.

The first European known to have landed in Australia was the Dutch sailor Willem Janszoon, who stepped ashore in 1606, and on European maps for two centuries, the continent was named New Holland. But the Dutch found nothing on the bleak northwestern coast to excite their commercial instincts, and the first explorer to look

A detail from a painting of a tribal celebration shows two Aborigines clad in animal skins clapping boomerangs beneath spiny anteaters. The artist, William Barak, was the last survivor of his tribe, whose territory in Victoria in southeast Australia was purchased by a European settler in 1835 for some blankets, shirts, knives, and mirrors. From the 1860s, Barak painted a number of similar scenes to satisfy the curiosity of white colonists concerning the culture that they had displaced.

111

upon Australia with covetous eyes was the British mariner James Cook. In 1770, Cook formally declared possession of the eastern coast—which he named New South Wales—in the name of King George III, and his impressions were very different: He saw vast numbers of whales and seals that might be exploited, he believed the area would provide a base for trade with the Far East, and he anticipated a regular supply of timber, flax, hemp, and pitch, all essential in large quantities for the Royal Navy.

But Britain was preoccupied with rebellion in its American colonies, and it was scarcely eager to embark on a fresh colonial venture. After a bitter war, the Americans won their independence; and Britain, which had previously shipped its unwanted criminals across the Atlantic, looked to Australia for an alternative dumping-ground.

In the years following their landfall at Sydney Cove in January 1788, many of the first British convicts to arrive in Australia probably wished they had chosen to be

The British settlement of Australia began and remained most concentrated in the southeastern sector *(right)*, where the climate and terrain were most hospitable. Coastal towns in other regions were founded by both private and government-sponsored ventures, but they remained isolated by vast distances—more than 2,000 miles separated Perth from Sydney on opposite sides of the continent. The map below shows the borders and capitals of the six colonies that joined together in 1901 to form the federated Commonwealth of Australia.

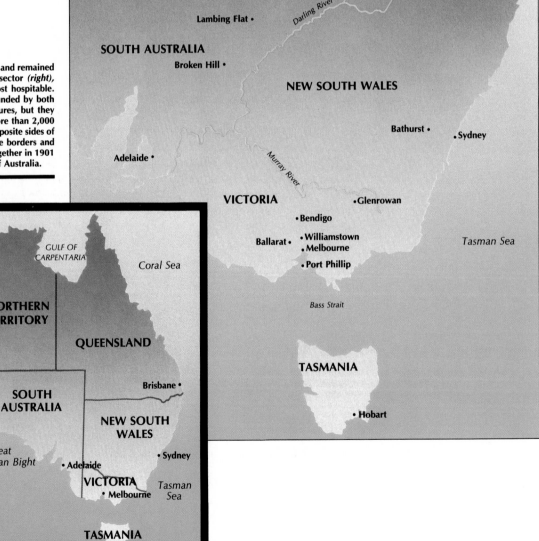

hanged by the neck rather than transported to the other side of the world. Most were diseased, illiterate, and lacking in any knowledge of agriculture. They suffered famine, drought, and ferocious punishments at the hands of their military guards. The governor, Arthur Phillip, soon called for free immigrants with farming skills, but it proved difficult at first to attract them: The best yeoman farmers were already doing perfectly well in England, and those who did decide to emigrate usually preferred to go to America, because it was nearer and the passage was cheaper.

Gradually, conditions in Australia improved. By 1792, when ill health forced Phillip to return to England, his settlement in New South Wales had become almost self-supporting, no longer wholly dependent on supplies sent from England. In 1802 and 1803, the circumnavigation of Australia by a naval officer named Matthew Flinders confirmed that the isolated stretches of coastline already charted belonged

In a watercolor-and-ink drawing executed in the 1840s, a convict superintendent, his wife, and her niece observe prisoners at work on a government farm in Tasmania, known as Van Diemen's Land until 1855. After working for some eighteen months on projects that included land clearing and the building of roads and bridges, most prisoners were released to find paid employment. Local free settlers resented the competition, and the transportation of British convicts to Australia was finally ended in 1868.

to a single landmass, and this foreshadowed Britain's territorial claim over the whole continent. New settlements were founded at Port Phillip, near the later site of Melbourne, and in Tasmania. An expedition across the Blue Mountains west of Sydney in 1813 opened up grazing land for the growing flocks of sheep, whose wool—along with some whaling and sealing—soon became the mainstay of the economy.

Four years later, returning from an expedition west of the grazing lands, a disappointed explorer concluded that "for all practical purposes of civilized man, the interior of this country, westward of the 147th meridian, is uninhabitable." This was not true, of course: The entire continent had been home for at least 50,000 years to

Australia's Aborigines, and it was they who paid the price for the white colonists' advances. The first settlers, following the lead of Governor Phillip, had been scrupulous in their dealings with the indigenous people, but friction between two vastly different cultures was inevitable. The Aborigines were hunter-gatherers, and it seemed only natural to them to spear a sheep for food whenever they needed one—an attitude that did not commend itself to hard-pressed sheep farmers, who could see their livelihood dwindling away. Atrocities against Aborigines became commonplace, one of the most notorious being the murder of twenty-eight men, women, and children at Myall Creek in 1838. Seven men were hanged for their part in this massacre; they freely admitted that they had killed the Aborigines but claimed that their actions were not criminal, as they regarded their victims as less than human.

In all, as many as 20,000 Aborigines were killed by white settlers. Many more died from diseases to which they had no immunity, and as they became dispersed and dispossessed of their lands, their birthrate plummeted. Between 1788 and 1900, their population fell from at least 750,000 to around 100,000.

The momentum of development was sustained in the 1830s and 1840s by the arrival of large numbers of free immigrants. In 1829 and 1836, two private colonizing ventures—similar to those that had established British settlements in North America in the seventeenth century—founded the colonies of Western and South Australia, with their capital towns of Perth and Adelaide. The new dependencies—such as Victoria, which separated from New South Wales—had almost no convicts, and the transportation of convicts to New South Wales ceased in 1840. The British government acceded to demands by the free settlers for their own representative assemblies, and New South Wales elected its first colonial legislature in 1842. Victoria, South Australia, and Tasmania followed in 1850, and Queensland in 1859.

In all six colonies, the new waves of immigrants expanded the areas of settlement. Hardy pioneers drove their sheep into unclaimed land; they were dubbed squatters by those who had paid for their property, but their success soon robbed this word of its derogatory overtones. The sheep-based economy progressed by leaps and bounds: By 1850, Britain was importing 38.8 million pounds of wool annually from Australia—more than five times the amount it was receiving from Germany, its previous chief supplier. Halfway through the century, the colonists' hold was secure. Many had been born in Australia and knew no other home. But none foresaw the riches that were about to be discovered, or the rapid changes their communities would experience.

A stubborn opportunist, Edward Hargraves of New South Wales had put his hand to many jobs: farmer, sailor, innkeeper, shipping agent, and in 1849, when he traveled to the gold fields of California, prospector. Back in Australia, with no more in his pocket than when he had set out, he recalled a shallow creek near Bathurst, across the Blue Mountains, that was similar to the locations where gold had been found in California, and he determined to try his luck once more. On the morning of February 12, 1851, Hargraves—dressed, according to one report, in top hat and tails, for he was fully aware of the momentous significance of what he might find—filled his tin dish with some handfuls of soil, washed away the sand, and saw at last what two years before he had crossed the world to look for: Gold!

News of the find aroused alarm as well as excitement. The leading Sydney news-

Maintaining their dignity despite their desolation, Tasmanian Aborigines *(right)* pose for the camera in 1858. By 1847, when they were moved to a settlement at Oyster Bay near Hobart, their numbers had diminished from about 7,000 at the start of the century to just 47. Most succumbed to disease or drink; the last full-blood survivor, a woman named Truganini, died in 1876.

paper hoped "that the treasure does not exist in large quantities," for if it did, Australia was on course for "calamities far more terrible than earthquakes and pestilence." But when a nugget weighing almost ninety pounds was discovered in a block of quartz, and when even richer strikes were made at Ballarat and Bendigo, sixty-two miles from Melbourne, nothing could stop the lightning spread of gold fever.

All over the continent, from Sydney in the east to Perth in the west, from the streets of Melbourne to the sheep stations of New South Wales, men of all classes from landowners to domestic servants dropped whatever they were doing, abandoned their homes and families, and hurried to the gold fields. They were joined by prospectors from abroad, who invested all their savings in the long sea voyage to Australia. In 1852, the number of immigrants increased sevenfold to 95,000; over the following ten years, the country's population was to triple to 1.2 million.

Most of the immigrants came from Great Britain, but many came from America too, from the California gold fields, and later from China, as the demand for unskilled labor outstripped supply. To the Australian squatter of an earlier, land-seeking generation was added a new character, the "digger"—the determined prospector whose single aim was to get rich quick, and who cared nothing about the background or

In a study executed by Thomas Baines, a member of an expedition into the interior of northern Australia in 1855, an Aborigine with his barbed spear rests against a tree *(opposite)*. In regions remote from the colonized southeastern corner of the continent, Aborigines maintained a way of life largely unchanged for tens of thousands of years. The men hunted kangaroos and emus with spears and boomerangs; the women gathered seeds, roots, honey, and fruit and caught small animals such as lizards and frogs.

antecedents of his fellow miners. It was against this backdrop that the transportation of convicts to Australia was finally abandoned, for a free passage to the promised land, under the circumstances, was scarcely a punishment at all.

But the anxieties expressed by the Sydney newspaper were well founded. Gold brought prosperity to Australia, but it also brought social upheaval, as the labor force headed for the gold fields and farms were left untended. The authorities were ill prepared for the sudden influx of immigrants, and their efforts to police the new

mining settlements—an unpopular job, often undertaken by ex-convicts—and to set up at least the rudiments of government control provoked unrest. The expense of managing the gold fields was passed on to the miners in the form of a license fee, which successful and unsuccessful miners alike were required to pay. The police took a commission on every fee collected, and those who could not or would not pay were treated as criminals. The miners came to resent the police bitterly.

They developed other grievances too. The miners in Victoria were making the colony rich, but because they did not own property, they did not have the right to vote in elections for the colony's legislature. And those who wanted to invest their earnings in land discovered that prices were escalating. From the police, the administration, and the landowners, the miners felt they were getting a raw deal.

Conflict came to a head in Ballarat in 1854, when a drunken miner named James Scobie got into a quarrel with a hotelkeeper and his strong-arm man, a former policeman, and was later found dead in unexplained circumstances. It was obvious to the miners that the two men had beaten Scobie to death, but the magistrates refused to send the case to trial, and the culprits were set free. The miners had seen bribery and corruption before, but this time they decided that enough was enough.

First they burned down the hotel. Then they held a series of mass meetings, at which the issue of Scobie's death was rapidly swallowed up in a general demand for the redress of grievances. On November 11, some 10,000 diggers voted to set up a reform league to agitate for an extensive political program. Their strongest demands were for new management for the gold fields and the cancellation of the hated license fee; but they also called for full manhood suffrage, regular elections, salaries for members of the legislative council, and the abolition of a property-owning qualification for political candidates.

The Melbourne administration responded by sending more troops to the gold fields and by redoubling its efforts to collect the fees. The diggers made a huge pile of their licenses and ceremonially burned them. A riot followed, and the more extreme diggers began to erect a defensive stockade at Eureka, near the site of the burned-down hotel. Egged on by their leaders, they took a solemn oath of loyalty and defied the authorities to do their worst.

On Sunday morning, December 3, the commander of the surrounding troops called on the 150 miners within the stockade to surrender. When they refused, he ordered his men to charge. Within a quarter of an hour, twenty-five diggers lay dead

With supplies roped to ox-drawn carts, teamsters prepare to set out for an isolated sheep station. On the return journey, the carts will be stacked high with bales of wool. As pastures for grazing sheep or cattle spread into the interior during the latter half of the nineteenth century, an intense camaraderie developed among the teamsters, shearers, and drovers who traversed the vast distances between remote stations and the coastal ports. Their staple food was often damper, an unleavened bread cooked in a cast-iron pot buried in a hole filled with hot coals. In the inset above, drovers clutching mugs of tea eagerly await their morning ration.

Woolsorters pause for the photographer in their work-shed in New South Wales. Newly sheared fleeces were spread out on slatted tables to be sorted into grades of fineness; they were then pressed into bales and shipped to textile mills, mostly in Britain. The finest wool was produced by the Spanish merino sheep, the first specimens of which were imported in 1797. By 1890, there were 100 million sheep on the continent.

and more than fifty were wounded, against five soldiers dead and twelve wounded.

The miners had been routed, but the moral victory was undoubtedly theirs. The authorities reacted to the disaster by granting the miners most of what they had asked for. The license fee was abolished, to be replaced by a much cheaper miner's "right," which also entitled the holder to vote in Victoria's elections. The administration of the gold fields was reorganized, and the necessary revenue was raised by a new export tax on gold. These measures were seen as a great victory for the workingman, and the heroes of the Eureka stockade were celebrated in ballad and song.

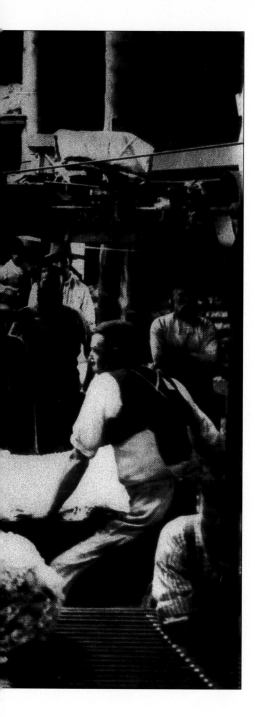

But not all the miners' grievances were satisfied, for they now felt threatened by the thousands of Chinese laborers who were imported to work in the mines in response to declining profits. The Chinese worked hard for low wages and sent a large proportion of their money home rather than investing it in Australia. The miners petitioned the parliaments of Victoria and New South Wales, which in due course passed a series of laws discriminating against the Chinese already in the gold fields and severely restricting further immigration.

The Chinese began to enter South Australia instead, whence they walked overland in groups of several hundred. They were met with open hostility. The situation reached the boiling point in 1861 at Lambing Flat in New South Wales, where the Chinese community numbered around 1,500. On Sunday, June 30, a mob of 3,000 white colonists, armed with staves and pick handles, swarmed into the Chinese camp, burning the tents and humiliating the Chinese by cutting off their pigtails. The police and the army made a delayed arrival, and at a trial of the ringleaders, all those charged with rioting were found not guilty. The Chinese were understandably dismayed. The gold fields offered opportunities to all, but to some more than others.

Although many foreign prospectors went home after the gold rush was over, hundreds of thousands stayed, and their need for housing, work, and land posed severe problems for the colonial governments. Most of the politicians were inexperienced and lacked any tradition of public service. As a result, the political parties in each colony tended to promote the local, short-term interests of their supporters rather than work for the common good. But, by gradual stages, reforms were set in motion.

Housing problems were most acute in the overcrowded cities, where poverty and sweated labor were the norm for the working classes. The population of Melbourne had grown from 39,000 to 140,000 in just ten years, and it was common in the 1860s for a family of fourteen to be squeezed into two rooms, each measuring less than six feet by six feet. But those living outside the cities fared little better. Whole families were brought up in bark huts with earthen floors, using sacking for beds and wooden crates for furniture. During the 1860s, about one-fifth of the European population of eastern Australia was living under canvas or in temporary accommodations.

Extensive building programs alleviated the plight of the homeless and transformed the appearance of the cities. The newly prosperous middle classes, solidly rooted in the same values of property, hard work, and self-improvement that characterized the well-to-do of Victorian Britain, built comfortable suburban homes, often decorated with ornate ironwork known as Sydney lace, and frequented public buildings that were constructed in a distinctly baroque style. In Melbourne, the English architect Joseph Reed, having failed to make a fortune in the gold fields, made his name instead as the designer of the town hall, the trades hall, and various banks and churches. His buildings were solid, sober, and secure, and they were often crowned with a baroque dome, the ultimate symbol of a confident and assured society.

Outside the cities, however, opportunities to earn a secure livelihood were still scarce. All the best farming land had been appropriated by the squatters in the first half of the century, and when land did occasionally come up for sale, its price was far beyond the means of the recent immigrants. It soon became clear that the situation would have to be remedied—although exactly how, nobody could agree. The newcomers argued that in this young and forward-looking country, where birth and hereditary status counted for little, the land must be unlocked to provide equal opportunities for all. But the squatters insisted that what was theirs was theirs and could not be taken away from them.

Land-hungry citizens began to agitate for reform and to marshal impressive statistics to support their case. They pointed out that in Victoria, for instance, the 30.9 million acres in the hands of the squatters did not even make the colony self-sufficient in food. Sheep there were in plenty—tens of millions over the whole continent, rising to 100 million by 1890—but sheep were not enough. The richest agricultural land was not being put to proper use.

The sheep farmers replied that wool was Australia's most important export, a mainstay of the economy, and used their influence in the colonial parliaments to argue that throwing the land open to all and sundry would lead to all sorts of problems, from overproduction and undercapitalization to inefficiency and economic ruin. But their arguments were in vain, and one by one, the parliaments

Bark-roofed huts on a hillside in New South Wales cover mine shafts dug by gold-hungry prospectors *(above)*. Ore and rock were raised from the mines by horse-powered winches. Hoping to make a quick fortune, the diggers cared little for safety or comfortable living conditions, but they bitterly resented the license fees exacted by the colonial authorities. The painting on the right depicts troops storming a stockaded camp at Eureka in Victoria after miners had burned their licenses and refused to surrender.

capitulated. Laws passed during the 1860s in New South Wales, Victoria, Queensland, and South Australia all made land available to anyone who could pay a small deposit—with the balance to be paid off without interest over the following years—on the sole condition that this land was to be used for growing crops.

The aim was to make the land available to the poor rather than the rich, but the results varied widely from colony to colony. In New South Wales, possession of the prime grazing lands was fiercely disputed between squatters and would-be purchasers. Bribery, physical violence, and dummying—getting friends and relations to take up their entitlements on one's behalf—were everyday occurrences. It was common, too, for squatters to put their holdings into an anonymous company and then apply for new land under their own names. Elsewhere the system worked slightly better. In Victoria—where some 30,000 people had purchased small holdings by 1869—and in South Australia, large amounts of land changed hands. But the new owners did not always fare as well as they had hoped. Every year between 1862 and 1870 saw either a drought or a flood. The disasters forced many of the impoverished farm owners to mortgage their holdings to banks or to give up altogether.

Transport was a further problem. Distances were great and the roads poor; many farmers were unable to get their produce to a market. The first railway line had been built between Williamstown and Melbourne in Victoria in 1854, but over the next twenty years, less than 1,000 miles of new track were laid. Because of a lack of coordination among the colonies, many of the lines had different gauges, with results that bedeviled the country for more than a century; some of the colonies also set up counterproductive tariffs against one another rather than coming to a common agreement over trade policies.

Not until the 1870s did the colonial governments, supported by British investors, initiate a large program of public works, including the construction of an additional 10,000 miles of railroad track. The railways were followed in turn by trading posts, telegraph wires, and other trappings of progress. The wire fence especially was a great boon to Australia, because its use—in place of the more expensive post and rail—meant that vast areas of land could be cheaply enclosed and sheep prevented from wandering. By the end of the 1870s, most of Victoria, New South

ISLANDS OF THE MAORI

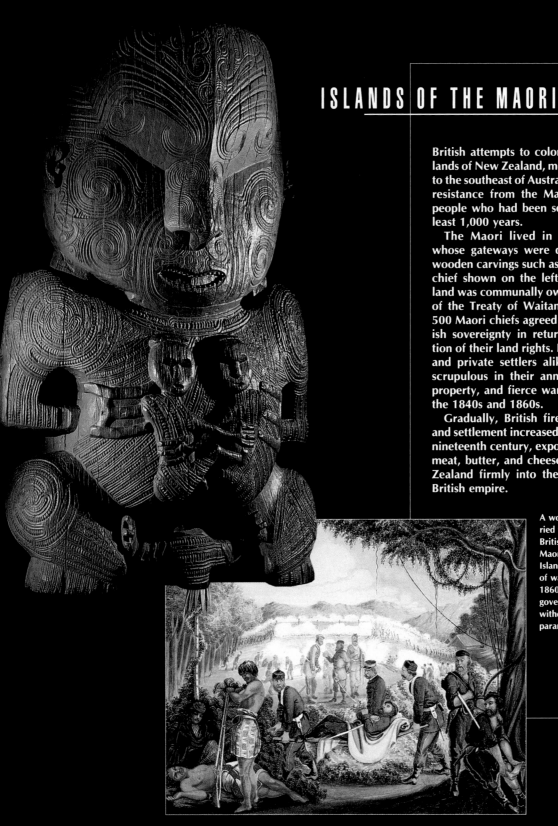

British attempts to colonize the fertile islands of New Zealand, more than 900 miles to the southeast of Australia, met with stern resistance from the Maori, a Polynesian people who had been settled there for at least 1,000 years.

The Maori lived in fortified villages whose gateways were decorated by fine wooden carvings such as that of a tattooed chief shown on the left; the surrounding land was communally owned. By the terms of the Treaty of Waitangi in 1840, some 500 Maori chiefs agreed to recognize British sovereignty in return for the protection of their land rights. But administrators and private settlers alike were far from scrupulous in their annexation of Maori property, and fierce warfare broke out in the 1840s and 1860s.

Gradually, British firepower prevailed, and settlement increased. By the end of the nineteenth century, exports of refrigerated meat, butter, and cheese had bound New Zealand firmly into the economy of the British empire.

A wounded soldier is carried from the battlefield as British troops storm a Maori village on North Island in 1866. A decade of warfare began here in 1860, when the British governor tried to buy land without the consent of the paramount Maori chief.

Wales, and Queensland were fenced, and an ambitious series of irrigation projects along the Murray River had enabled marginal land to be economically cultivated. Australians were learning that they did not need to strike gold to become rich, and that efficient management could make their land an equally valuable resource.

From the very beginning, Australia was an intensely masculine society, much of its energy fueled by a need to believe that the hardy pioneer wresting a livelihood from the wilderness was equal to, if not better than, the educated dandy in the drawing rooms of far-off London. High among the qualities it demanded of its heroes were strength, the courage to challenge the brute elements, and the determination to live by one's own lights irrespective of the demands of established authority.

The most demanding testing ground for these qualities was the outback, the desert interior, whose emptiness was a constant challenge to land-hungry pioneers. In 1860, hoping to open up new grazing lands in uncharted territory, the government of Victoria announced a cash prize for the first south-to-north crossing of Australia. On August 20, a crowd of 15,000 gathered in Melbourne to witness the departure of an expedition of twelve men, with twenty-five camels specially imported from India; it was led by Robert O'Hara Burke, a daredevil Irishman who had little experience of exploration, and William John Wills, an English surveyor, both of whom had arrived in Australia as gold-seeking immigrants during the 1850s. There had been other explorers before them—notably Charles Sturt, who in 1844 had penetrated the interior as far as the Simpson Desert, and Ludwig Leichhardt, who had vanished without trace in 1848—but the names of Burke and Wills were to pass into legend.

The plan was to traverse the continent by stages, with an advance party setting out each day to prepare a camp where it would wait for the rest of the expedition and the supplies. But at Cooper's Creek, less than halfway across Australia, the impatient Burke decided to abandon the bulk of the supplies and proceed ahead with Wills and two companions, Charles Gray and John King. Journeying across the arid deserts of the interior, where temperatures could reach as high as 130° F. at noon and fall below zero at night, Burke's party eventually reached the tidal waters of the Flinders River, close to the Gulf of Carpentaria on Australia's northern coast, in February 1861. With their mission accomplished, the four men embarked on the return journey.

Two months later, having run out of supplies, Burke, Wills, and King staggered into the camp at Cooper's Creek, some 1,000 miles south of the gulf; Gray had died en route. Just a few hours before they arrived, the camp had been abandoned by the other members of the expedition. Burke wrote a message—"We proceed on tomorrow slowly down the creek to Adelaide, but we are very weak"—and buried this note in a bottle under a tree. He and King began walking south, but two days later Burke died of exhaustion. King returned to Cooper's Creek to find Wills also dead. By the time a search party arrived, the bodies of Burke and Wills had been reduced to skeletons; King had been rescued by a group of Aborigines, with whom he was living.

The fate of the explorers stirred the imagination of all their countrymen. The following December, the leader of the search party reported that "no less than five artists have commenced grand historical pictures of me burying Burke." Elegies were written, monuments were erected, and the remains of the two pioneers were brought back to Melbourne and given Victoria's first state funeral, in January 1862.

Burke and Wills were deemed to have given their lives for the public good, and in 1864, a massive bronze statue of them was unveiled by the governor of Victoria. But

the Australian people cared little for such official blessings and bestowed their affection equally upon some of the roughest outlaws of the period. These were the bushrangers—frontier bandits who roamed the sparsely populated regions on the fringe of the outback, stealing horses and robbing mail coaches at will. Many of the earliest bushrangers were escaped convicts; from the 1860s, most were native-born Australians who simply chose the outlaw's life as the easiest route to riches.

The bushrangers' ability to outwit the police, who were hindered by poor roads and communications as well as their own incompetence, made them popular with those who had suffered from police brutality. Many homesteaders in outlying areas did not share these sentiments, but they remained silent for fear of reprisals. Books, plays, and ballads commemorated these unlikely heroes, and young boys played games modeled upon their exploits. The most famous bushranger was Ned Kelly, a small-time cattle thief who graduated to bank robbery and murder, boasting all the while that he and his gang had never harmed a woman or robbed a poor man. Such claims were untrue, but they won Kelly a Robin Hood status among many of the poor and dispossessed. Kelly was eventually run to ground in 1880 in the town of Glenrowan in Victoria. Despite petitions bearing tens of thousands of signatures that pleaded for his pardon, he was hanged in Melbourne in November at the age of twenty-five.

Kelly was the last of his kind, for bushrangers could not thrive in a world of railroads and the electric telegraph. By 1880, native-born Australians outnumbered immigrants, and their country was entering a new era: Its economy was expanding, and its people were acquiring new preoccupations and a new idea of their status in the world. Some of the confidence engendered by material prosperity would prove unfounded, but enough would remain to carry the colonists through temporary crises and on to a full realization of their continent's potential.

During the late 1870s and the 1880s, the British saw Australia as an ideal investment opportunity, and the Australians eagerly agreed. Moreover, they now had new sources of income of their own, for quantities of copper had been found in Queensland, and a seemingly endless supply of silver, lead, and zinc was discovered at Broken Hill in New South Wales. The coal mines were flourishing—tripling their output in twenty years to supply the new trains and steamships—while experiments with agriculture led to a drought-resistant strain of wheat and established the viability of the sugarcane industry in the subtropical climate of northern Queensland.

Ordinary working people profited no less than the big farmers and business entrepreneurs from this economic boom, and trade unions emerged as a powerful voice in Australian politics. Skilled laborers, in short supply during the first half of the century, had been able to command high wages and had formed craft associations to press home their advantage. By 1855, stonemasons, carpenters, and other workers in the building trade in Melbourne had achieved their demands for an eight-hour day, and in 1870, the unions were granted legal recognition. More trades and labor councils were established during the 1870s, and in 1879, the first intercolonial union congress was held at Sydney. The Amalgamated Miners' Union and the Shearers' Union both pushed successfully for improvements in working conditions to match those of their colleagues in the older unions, and committees in the colonial parliaments lobbied for the right to strike.

The English novelist Anthony Trollope, who visited Australia in 1872, had no doubt that the lot of the working classes was far better in Australia than it was in England. He found that the typical worker was "better fed than the laborer at home, better housed, better clothed, and is therefore more of a man." Of Melbourne he enthused: "There is perhaps no town in the world in which an ordinary workingman can do better for himself. He not only lives better with more comfortable appurtenances around him, but he fills a higher position in regard to those around him and has greater consideration paid to him than would have fallen to his lot at home." As such news spread abroad, Australia became known as the "workingman's paradise."

Australia's economic progress was matched by advances in many other fields. The cultural life of its cities was enriched by the poems, plays, and novels of writers who took as their themes the struggles of the early immigrants and the hardships of life in the bush. Landscape painters made the untamed wilderness vivid for an urbanized society. Students entered the universities of Sydney and Melbourne, founded in the 1850s, in increasing numbers, and a new university opened in Adelaide in 1875. In sports, Australian cricketers had the satisfaction of defeating an English team in Melbourne, and five years later, they repeated their victory in London. These achievements contributed to a sense of national identity. Australians remained intensely loyal to Queen and Empire (their troops fought bravely in the Sudan in 1885, and in the Boer War) but gave their loyalty as an independent people, with hearts and minds of their own.

This crude suit of armor, fashioned out of plowshares, was worn by the bank robber Ned Kelly during his shootout with the police at Glenrowan, Victoria, in June 1880. The other members of his gang were burned to death when the hotel in which they were hiding was set on fire. Striding alone toward his attackers, Kelly was brought down by shots in his foot, hand, and arm. A few months later he was tried and hanged.

But Australia's very success gave rise to new conflicts and reactivated old ones. It was as if the country had progressed too far too fast. One issue that divided the colonies and set unions against employers was the importation of some 50,000 people from the South Sea Islands to the sugar plantations of northern Queensland. The planters insisted that white people were not suitable for this type of work, but the use of colored laborers as a cheap work force proved unpopular both with the unions—who denounced it as little more than slave trade—and with the other colonies, which had enacted laws to discourage colored immigration. The islanders faced the same hostility and prejudice the Chinese had endured two decades before.

More ominous still, the foundations of Australia's prosperity were not as secure as they seemed. Collectively, the colonists had borrowed more than £200 million during the boom, mostly from Britain, and much was invested unwisely. In the cities, officials and private citizens used it to erect grandiose buildings; in the country, it served to bring unsuitable land into cultivation, as farmers borrowed heavily in the

A painting of Melbourne, capital of Victoria, in 1861 by Henry Burn shows citizens promenading on a wide street beneath a skyline dominated by English-style neo-Gothic church towers and spires *(opposite)*. The first houses were built in 1837, two years after the land had been bought from the Aborigines. By 1900, the city was the most populous in Australia, with some half million inhabitants. Many of the more prosperous lived in detached suburban villas similar to those depicted above in an architect's design.

hope that the rains would come and transform scrub into an oasis.

Nemesis was inevitable. In 1890, a financial crisis in Argentina led to the failure of a major London bank, which had a sobering effect on other banks, both British and Australian. The consequences for investment in Australia were little short of disastrous. In the same year, disputes between unions and employers came to a head over the dismissal of a union official on the steamship *Corinna* on Sydney's waterfront. Fellow employees promptly went on strike, to be joined—in a typical display of mateship—by an even larger number of miners and sheepshearers. By mid-September, some 50,000 men had laid down their tools. The country was in chaos.

Six weeks later, the authorities could claim a victory. Public opinion was overwhelmingly on the side of the employers; faced with such opposition, the strikers capitulated. But that was not the end of the troubles for business, for the strikes were followed by an economic slump. The unions were widely blamed, but the root of the problem was the loss of business confidence in the wake of the Argentinian default. More than forty land and finance companies failed in Melbourne and Sydney in 1891 and 1892, and all public works and most private building came to an abrupt halt. The banks raised interest rates to keep English investment flowing, but panic-stricken depositors began to withdraw their funds. In January 1893, the Federal Bank closed its doors and suspended all trading; soon another twelve banks took similar action.

The situation was worst in Victoria, where Melbourne never recovered its preeminence as Australia's financial center, but the other colonies suffered too. New South Wales was cushioned by its wool economy, but the depression was severe nonetheless and led to extensive unemployment. Its effects were felt all over the country, coming as a shock to people who had believed the good times would last forever.

This blow to Australia's buoyant self-confidence focused the attention of many on the possible advantages of federation—a full union of the six colonies into one country. The idea had first been proposed fifty years earlier but had never gained widespread support. But in the 1890s, two pressing arguments for federation emerged. First, it appeared that the colonies were no longer capable of confronting economic crises on their own. And second, Australians were becoming increasingly aware that rivalries between the colonial powers of Europe posed a potential threat to their shores. In 1853, France had occupied the island of New Caledonia, just ten days' sail from Australia; in 1884, Germany annexed part of New Guinea; in 1887,

France and Britain took over joint administration of the New Hebrides; and it was conjectured in several newspapers that, in the event of a war in Europe, Russia would try to invade Australia. The last British troops to be garrisoned in Australia had left in 1870. If the colonies were to have any chance of resisting an invasion, it was clear that they would have to pool their meager military resources.

Support for federation was far from unanimous. The middle classes were mostly in favor of abolishing intercolonial tariffs, and of establishing a strong central executive to curb the unions. The latter were less enthusiastic, fearing a strong alliance between the authorities and the employers. A New South Wales politician remarked that federation would mean that his colony, the only one favoring free trade, would be placed in the position of a sober man cohabiting with five drunkards. Those who lived in the outback tended to support federation, which they saw as a blow against the vested interests of the big cities; many city dwellers naturally held opposing views. The more the issues were discussed, the more divided the Australians became.

But the idea of federation had taken root, and in 1895, the colonial premiers decided that proposals for a federal constitution should be drawn up by representatives from each of the six colonies. At a yearlong series of conventions that opened in March 1897, the details of this draft constitution were hammered out. It was proposed that the official head of state would remain the British sovereign, and the signature of her representative, the governor general, would be required to validate all legislation. But government would essentially be directed by two houses of Parliament—the Senate, to which the six states would each elect six members; and the House of Representatives, to be elected by universal manhood suffrage. (Women were to be given the vote—which they already had in two colonies—in 1902.) Finally, it was agreed that a new capital city should be built in New South Wales.

After two national referendums, Western Australia still refused to accept these proposals, but a compromise was finally reached, and delegates from all the colonies traveled to London to present their bill to the British government. They got a friendly reception. The territories of the British empire were far from uniform, and the government's policies toward them varied: Over countries acquired by conquest, it retained absolute control, but in lands settled by voluntary migration, it had been prepared from an early stage to grant a measure of self-government. Canada had been granted autonomy in 1867. Besides, the government was loath to alienate the Australian people while their troops were fighting alongside the British in the Boer War.

Queen Victoria gave her assent to the new constitution in September 1900, and on New Year's Day in 1901 the Commonwealth of Australia came into being. The parties had begun the previous night. "Never was a moonlit midnight in Sydney marked by a wilder, more prolonged, or generally more discordant welcome," reported Alfred Deakin, Australia's first attorney general. "All music was lost in the tumultuous uproar of the streets, where whistles, bells, gongs, accordions, rattles, and clanging culinary utensils yielded unearthly sounds."

The four and a half million citizens of Australia certainly had much to celebrate. Hardy individualists working in towns and on farmsteads separated by vast distances, they had made the bleak terrain of their isolated continent bear fruit, and over a period of just a few generations, they had transformed a geographical entity into a political one. As a dominion of the British empire, their country was still subordinate to the British Crown in matters of defense and foreign relations; but in all other spheres, Australians had taken their destiny into their own hands.

In a detail from a painting by Tom Roberts, a stockman strives to head off a stampede of sheep in the fierce, hot glare of a January day. The painting was executed in 1891, a year in which much of Australia was preoccupied with industrial unrest and the first signs of an economic depression. Incorporating outdated details such as the log fence—widely replaced by barbed wire during the 1880s—Roberts's picture evoked a bygone era of rugged individualism, seen as a vanished golden age.

AMERICA DIVIDED

On a spring day in 1848, the inhabitants of the small California settlement of San Francisco were bemused by the spectacle of an excited shopkeeper running through the muddy streets, brandishing a bottle filled with something shiny, and bellowing "Gold! Gold! Gold!" Sam Brannan, who sold supplies to the lumberjacks and settlers in the lower Sacramento Valley, was not the first to bring back word of the amazing discovery: The workers building a new sawmill on the American River had spotted the glitter of gold nuggets on the site back in January, and—in spite of their boss's efforts to keep the news under wraps until his mill was complete—the story had trickled out. But now, as the weather warmed and Brannan waved his hat at the crowd of curious onlookers, the fever struck.

Farmers and artisans dropped whatever they were doing and headed for the American River. Schoolteachers dismissed their classes; merchants closed up shop and left signs on the doors of their abandoned premises: "Gone to the diggings." The excitement soon spread far beyond the California Territory, which had been formally acquired by the United States only months before as the spoils of a war against their Mexican neighbors. Around two-thirds of the able-bodied male population in the adjacent Oregon Territory flooded south to the new gold fields, where they were soon joined by adventurers from the eastern part of the United States, from South America, and even from Europe. Jolting in wooden wagons along the overland trails across the western wilderness, or making the long, costly journey by sea, 80,000 arrived in the course of a single year.

In the early days, some adventurers made spectacular strikes, earning themselves thousands of dollars in a matter of weeks. Most prospectors' finds were more modest, but still brought them more wealth than they could earn by any other honest means. The average find was approximately thirty grams of gold dust per day, worth twenty times the daily wage of a laborer back East.

The treasure seekers who flocked to the gold fields of California became known as forty-niners, from the year during which gold fever reached its peak. But the glitter of gold was not the only magnet that drew settlers westward across the great river valleys, prairies, deserts, and mountain ranges separating the settled states of the Union from the newly acquired stretch of the Pacific Coast. In 1845, a political journalist had prophesied "the fulfillment of our Manifest Destiny to overspread the continent allotted by Providence," and politicians of all parties had elevated this phrase into an article of faith.

By dint of negotiation, warfare, or the exercise of squatters' rights, the United States had gradually eased out France, Britain, Spain, and Mexico, the foreign powers that had once contended for the lands beyond the boundaries of the original thirteen states. In the northwest, Britain and the United States had agreed in 1846 to divide

In a detail from a painting by Samuel Colman, a wagon train fords the Medicine Bow River in Wyoming on its route across the Rocky Mountains. Through such idealized images, the hardy pioneer entered American folklore as an emblematic figure of the frontier territory of the West, alongside the stereotypes of the marauding Indian and the trigger-happy cowboy. By the end of the century, when the land had been transformed by commerce and urban development, these characters possessed the added appeal of nostalgia.

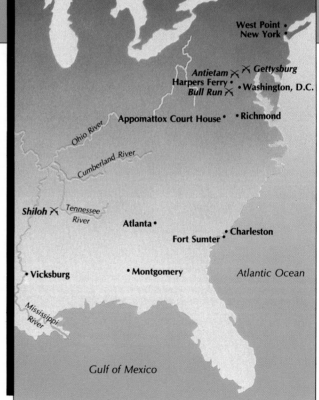

By 1861, the patchwork of new territories acquired by the Republic of the United States extended to the western edge of the continent *(above)*. In that year, irreconcilable differences between the largely agrarian South *(green)* and the industrialized North erupted into armed conflict in the eastern part of the nation *(inset, right)*. However, not even the trauma of the Civil War slowed the settlement of the western territories, whose borders were soon revised by the formation of new states of the Union.

the sprawling territory of Oregon along the forty-ninth parallel. Victory in the Mexican War had given the Republic control of Texas and New Mexico as well as California. Only the native Indian tribes now stood between settled eastern states and the Pacific Ocean in the West.

This expansionist momentum was to stir other, unpredictable currents within American society. The most damaging had its source in the quarrel between those states whose economy was based on the labor of black slaves and those that abhorred the practice of slavery. Little more than a decade after the California gold rush, the southern states in the eastern sector of the continent threatened to secede from the Union, and the armies of the southern and the northern states clashed in a momentous civil war that claimed more than 620,000 lives. But the outcome of this war ensured the unity of the Republic, and released new energies for the development of the western territories. By 1890, the resistance of the Indian tribes had been broken, and the "frontier"—the line defining the outer limit of settled territory—no longer existed. Thanks to massive capital investment in industry, transportation, and communications, the United States had succeeded in becoming the wealthiest country in the world. On both sides of the continent, its citizens looked out across the oceans with a proud and eager mien.

As the western perimeter of the Republic advanced from the Appalachians to the Mississippi Valley, and finally to the rim of the Pacific, the hunters, trappers, traders, and gold seekers who blazed the first trails were followed by a tide of land-hungry migrants. These would-be farmers—restless natives of the eastern states, ambitious newcomers from Europe—packed their families and their hopes into long, narrow, canvas-covered conveyances called prairie schooners and banded together into wagon trains for protection. The most affluent of the pioneers might possess three or four wagons, filled with tools, supplies, and furniture for their new homes in the West, as well as mattresses, cooking utensils, and whatever else could be fitted in to provide themselves with domestic comforts along the way. A cow, roped to the wagon, provided fresh milk, and the prudent pioneer housewife rapidly learned that the bumping of the wagon over rutted trails afforded an excellent means of churning a pail of cream into butter. Poorer migrants set out with only a single tarpaulin-topped cart, or even a wheelbarrow, laden with a few sacks of provisions, some tools, and perhaps a change of clothing.

Depending on the size of the equipage, the condition of the trail, and the weather, the travelers might expect to cover between one and a half to six miles in a day. Mud slides, or sometimes merely the steepness of the trail, often compelled travelers to jettison some of their possessions in order to keep the horses and wagons moving. But whatever the rigors of the trail, the worst problem often was simply the tedium of the months-long journey. "I can't see," complained one pioneer bound for California, "what God Almighty made so much land for!"

Among the earliest and most fiercely determined of those who braved the westward trek were the Mormons—members of the Church of Jesus Christ of Latter-day Saints, a new, made-in-the-U.S.A. version of the Christian faith. Persecuted for their beliefs, which included a return to the polygamous practices of the Biblical patriarchs, they were driven out of one state after another in the East by murderous mobs, and ultimately, their founder, Joseph Smith, was shot and killed by a mob in Illinois. In 1846, the Mormons embarked on a meticulously organized exodus to the desert wastes of

In the shallows of a mountain stream in California, a gaunt prospector watches for the glitter of yellow metal in his tin dish during the gold rush of 1849. Panning for gold in this way was a lengthy process, and miners soon developed more sophisticated devices such as a rocking wooden box with filters that trapped heavy particles as loose debris flowed out. By 1853, teams of miners were dissolving banks of gravel with high-pressure jets of water; the loosened rubble rushed downward into sluice boxes, where the gold was separated out.

the Great Salt Lake basin in present-day Utah. Spurred on by religious zeal and the administrative genius of their new leader, Brigham Young, they managed to survive two years of near-starvation, while they coaxed crops of grains and vegetables from the arid soil of their new homeland.

The author of an 1845 handbook for new settlers heading westward held out a glorious vision:

> One grand scene of continuous improvements, universal enterprise, and unparalleled commerce. . . . Those fertile valleys shall groan under the immense weight of their abundant products; those numerous rivers shall teem with countless steamboats. . . . The entire country will be everywhere intersected with turnpike roads, railroads, and canals.

The writer's dream was not long in coming true. To take advantage of the vast expanses of new territory, the nation's entrepreneurs, and the federal government itself, applied prodigious energy to the creation of a far-reaching transportation and communications network. New technologies accelerated the pace of travel over land and water: The paving technique known as macadamizing produced smooth-surfaced roads that could be traveled in all kinds of weather; powerful engines swiftly moved steamboats along navigable rivers and the newly cut canals that linked New

In a painting dated 1861, Southern gentry stroll by a tranquil river and peacocks strut on the lawn in front of a Louisiana mansion. Only a very small proportion of the Southern states' population of nine million could afford such a leisured existence: Most whites were poor farmers with just a few acres of land, and labor for the large tobacco, sugarcane, and cotton plantations was provided by nearly four million black slaves *(opposite)*.

A. Persac. 1861.

York with the Northwest—and sent trains packed with goods and passengers rattling across the landscape.

Iron bridges crossed the waterways, and mountains were pierced by powerful explosives to tunnel a passage for the trains. By 1850, American railroad companies had laid almost 8,700 miles of track throughout the continent; a mere decade later, rails spanned more than 30,000 miles, a network larger than all the rest of the world's rail systems combined. Freight that once would have taken nearly two months, for instance, to move from Cincinnati to New York, now could make the same journey in less than seven days' time. And, along a web of telegraph wires that followed the tracks laid down for the railroad, information moved at an even more prodigious speed. From 1844, the telegraph, developed by the U.S. inventor Samuel Morse, sent words and numbers—orders, prices, offers, and counteroffers—across the country almost instantaneously. It was by these methods—which were more powerful and enduring than armed conquest or diplomatic treaty, that the United States secured and controlled its vast transcontinental dominions.

As their farms and commercial ventures prospered, and their trading posts expanded into small towns, the new citizens of the West turned their attention to the

Crowds throng the New York Crystal Palace exhibition held in 1853 to celebrate the variety and abundance of America's manufactured goods, most of which were produced in the factories of the North. Foreign visitors were especially impressed by the quality of machine-made precision instruments such as locks, clocks, and firearms. Two years after the exhibition closed, the building burned to the ground in half an hour.

This photograph of Abraham Lincoln, taken two years after he was elected president in 1861, shows the strains of the daunting tasks he faced. Famed for his integrity and high ideals, he declared: "If slavery is not wrong, nothing is wrong." At the same time, he recognized that the Southern states "are just what we would be in their situation." As the North and the South began to split apart, it was his goal to reunite the Republic.

establishment of law and government. From Kansas to California, community leaders drafted their own constitutions in preparation for statehood. Between 1815 and 1850, the United States welcomed an average of one new state every three years. The rest of the world looked on with amazement as the nation grew into a giant: By the middle of the 1850s, the United States had outstripped Great Britain, its mother country, to become one of the three most populous nations in the Western world, surpassed only by France and Russia. In 1840, the United States was home to slightly more than 17 million people; by 1860, the number had swollen to nearly 31.5 million.

The greatest concentration of population was still centered in the crowded cities and burgeoning small towns of the North, the states above the Mason-Dixon Line—as the border between Pennsylvania and Maryland was known, after the names of the men who had surveyed it in the eighteenth century. The transport revolution had freed the rural hinterland from the struggle to maintain an inefficient subsistence economy: Farmers in Iowa or Missouri could now send their crops and livestock to distant markets and use the same means to obtain cheaply mass-produced goods from the mills and factories of New Jersey or Massachusetts. The cities of the North were the nerve centers not only of industrial production but of financial power. Here magnates and bankers congregated, joint ventures were negotiated, and investment decisions were made that would affect the lives of Americans hundreds of miles away.

The agrarian South produced 75 percent of the world's cotton supply and a hefty share of its tobacco. These, together with such locally important crops as South Carolina rice and sugar from southern Louisiana, provided the United States with three-fifths of its exports. But although the great patrician landowners of the Cotton Belt ruled their plantations with the autocracy of medieval barons, the region's small farmers enjoyed few of the opportunities for economic betterment that the more industrialized North provided. The South possessed few factories, attracted little investment, had no state school system, and was covered by only a small portion of the new rail and communications networks. And the manner in which the South produced its vital cash crops revealed a difference between itself and the North more profound than the presence or absence of major industries and urban centers. For the economy of the rural South was based, as it had been for 200 years, on the unpaid labor of black slaves.

To the southern farmer—whether a tenant farmer toiling alongside his single field hand, or the master of a plantation possessing several hundred slaves—the prospect of working the land without slave labor was unthinkable. Yet to Northerners, the possibility that the institution of slavery might be carried over into the new western territories was equally untenable. The conflict between these two views threatened to split America into separate countries.

In the North, opposition to slavery was on the rise. Many Northern whites were as racially prejudiced as their Southern counterparts; but, nurtured on the ideals of human rights and freedom that had inspired the founders of their republic, they repudiated the notion that one race should exercise total power over another. The degradations and injustices of a way of life in which human beings could be bought and sold as chattel were brought home to Northern city dwellers by antislavery literature such as Theodore Weld's much-reprinted 1839 bestseller *American Slavery As It Is* and Harriet Beecher Stowe's popular novel *Uncle Tom's Cabin,* published in 1852. These texts demonstrated that, while individual slaveholders might be kind, the

Guarded by a lone sentry, a tattered Confederate flag flies over the ruined parapet of Fort Sumter in South Carolina. The seizure of this stronghold in April 1861, two months after seven Southern states had declared their secession from the Union, marked the opening of Civil War hostilities. The soldier-artist Conrad Chapman made sketches for this painting while under fire from the Union ships in the background, sent to blockade the Southern coast.

system itself was inherently inhumane. Weld quoted typical advertisements from Southern newspapers: "Negroes for Sale. A Negro woman twenty-four years of age, and two children, one eight and the other three years old. To be sold separately or together as desired."

The opposition to slavery, however, was based as much on economic as on ethical grounds, especially when Northerners contemplated the western territories that were preparing for statehood. In these undeveloped regions, where there was so much work to be done and a perpetual shortage of hands to do it, settlers from the Northern

states feared that Southerners, bringing in slaves who labored without wages, would have an unfair competitive edge. Newcomers from the South, in turn, resisted the notion that they should be forced to change their ways; they were usually poorer than their Northern counterparts, and the slaves they brought with them might be their only economic resource.

In the United States Congress, representatives from both Northern and Southern states hotly debated the western territories' terms of entry into the Union. Radicals wanted slavery abolished altogether; their opponents insisted that the inhabitants of every new state should have the right to decide for themselves, by popular vote, whether or not to allow slavery within their boundaries. Divisions were not purely geographical: There were Southerners hostile to slavery, and Northerners who opposed any attempts on the part of the federal government to restrict the slavery system. Compromises were offered, reversed, and modified, through years of acrimonious argument and behind-the-scenes negotiation.

In 1854, the Kansas-Nebraska Bill gave every state and territory the freedom to choose for itself whether or not slavery was to be permitted. Within a year, this right of self-determination had spawned a crisis. The territory destined to become the state of Kansas was split down the middle between proslavery and antislavery factions. Two separate governments were formed, and violent elements on both sides launched raiding parties, started riots, and murdered prominent opponents.

The uproar spread east to the nation's capital, where Northern and Southern legislators exchanged a volley of recriminations over the issue known as Bleeding Kansas. In May 1856, Senator Charles Sumner of Massachusetts launched into a two-day diatribe against the proslavery faction in which he accused Southerners of engineering "the rape of a virgin territory, compelling it to the hateful embrace of slavery." Four days later, Sumner was set upon in the Senate chamber by South Carolina Representative Preston S. Brooks, the nephew of a senator whom Sumner had singled out for particular abuse. To avenge his uncle's honor, Brooks brutally assaulted the Northerner with a gold-topped cane, battering him with such violence that Sumner never fully recovered from his injuries. "I gave him about thirty first-rate stripes," Brooks later recalled. "Toward the last, he bellowed like a calf. I wore my cane out completely, but saved the head."

Antislavery legislators were appalled, but not surprised. Such behavior, they said, was typical of a Southern slaveholder, accustomed to wielding power with whip and chain. Their opponents could scarcely conceal their satisfaction. Brooks was lauded in many parts of the South as a hero, and showered with adulatory letters and gifts of gold-topped canes, to replace the one he had broken in the attack.

Slavery became the most highly charged issue dividing North and South. Compromise legislation such as the Fugitive Slave Law, designed to placate the South when California and other western territories entered the Union as free rather than slave states, attracted increasing hostility from abolitionists. The law declared that an escaped slave remained the possession of his or her owner, even if the fugitive managed to reach the free states in the North, and allowed slave owners to send agents in pursuit of their missing property. When, under the terms of this act, a captured runaway named Anthony Burns was sent back to the South through the northern city of Boston, citizens draped the town's buildings in black and set the church bells tolling. Troops lined the streets to prevent any attempt to rescue Burns before he could be put on a ship sailing south.

Field guns and munitions at the Union arsenal at City Point, Virginia, await transportation to the front line. The North's industrial strength gave the Union vast superiority in ordnance over the Confederates, who had to buy military supplies from France and Britain and then run the gantlet of the Union naval blockade.

Abolitionists were further enraged by an 1857 judicial decision on a crucial constitutional issue, based on the case of a slave named Dred Scott. Scott had been brought out of the South during the 1830s by his master, an army surgeon, and after living for many years in the North, he sued his master's widow to gain his freedom. A prolonged sequence of trials and appeals brought the case to the United States Supreme Court, the highest legal tribunal in the Republic. The court—which was dominated by a majority of Southern judges—ruled that Scott, as a member of the Negro race, was not a citizen, and therefore was not entitled to the protection of the United States Constitution.

In 1859, a militant opponent of slavery named John Brown led a band of five blacks and seventeen whites in an attack against the government arsenal at Harpers Ferry, Virginia. His aim was to capture enough arms and ammunition to trigger a widespread slave revolt. But the plot failed, and Brown was hanged. By many who shared his sympathies, he was hailed as a martyr; but to the South, John Brown was yet another example of the widening breach. Some Southerners now believed that the old Union had outlived its usefulness: North and South had become two separate countries, whose peoples had different attitudes, interests, and aspirations. Conventions were held in South Carolina, Georgia, and Mississippi to discuss the possibility of secession from the Republic. "We are either slaves in the Union," declared one separatist from Georgia, "or free men out of it!"

The presidential campaign of 1860 was played out against a backdrop of mounting tension. Two years earlier, the candidates had run against each other in the state of Illinois for a seat in the Senate. In that contest, Democrat Stephen Douglas, who was avowedly less an advocate of slavery itself than an opponent of the federal government's power to impose its will on individual states, had defeated his Republican opponent, Abraham Lincoln, a successful Illinois lawyer who ran on a strong antislavery ticket. Many Southerners now warned that if the Republicans were victorious, secession might be the only course open to them.

One month after Lincoln was elected president, the state of South Carolina announced its secession from the Union. Within a few weeks, Mississippi, Florida, Alabama, Georgia, Louisiana, and Texas followed suit. In many regions, the most militant separatists were not the conservative grandees who owned the great plantations, but the poorest subsistence farmers, who felt themselves disenfranchised and had practically nothing to lose.

Northerners questioned the right of these states to secede. "We must settle this question now," declared Lincoln, "whether in a free government the minority have the right to break up the government whenever they choose." In February of 1861, delegates from the seven seceded states gave their own answer: In Montgomery, Alabama, they drew up plans for a new Confederate States of America, with its own congress, constitution, and national government. The right of its citizens to possess slaves, and the second-class status of the Negro race, were the basic premises of the new republic. "Its cornerstone," declared Alexander Stephens, vice president of the Confederacy, "rests upon the great truth that the Negro is not equal to the white man; that slavery . . . is his natural and normal condition. This, our new government, is the first in the history of the world based upon this great physical, philosophical, and moral truth."

When the Confederate president-elect, Jefferson Davis, a former U.S. senator, emerged into the streets of Montgomery to address a jubilant crowd, a waiting band struck up a popular tune called "Dixie," which became the Confederacy's unofficial anthem. "The time for compromise," Davis declared, "has now passed! The South is determined to maintain her position, and make all who oppose her smell Southern powder and feel Southern steel!"

Davis's words were more than empty rhetoric. While the other Southern states agonized over the implications of secession, and Northerners debated whether or not to fight to keep the Union together, the Confederacy began making military preparations. Just before dawn on April 12, 1861, Southern forces bombarded the isolated United States Army garrison at Fort Sumter, South Carolina, battering the federal stronghold for thirty-three hours before its commander surrendered.

In response, President Lincoln called up 75,000 federal militiamen into temporary service, with the declared intention of suppressing the insurrection. Within a few weeks, the states of Virginia, Arkansas, North Carolina, and Tennessee declared their secessions and joined the South. Both Lincoln and Jefferson Davis now knew that they were embarked on more than a short-lived civil affray.

Neither contender in the conflict was well equipped to wage a war. The Union maintained only a small standing army, from which many Southern-born officers and men withdrew to join the Confederate forces when hostilities began. Officers who had trained at the U.S. Military Academy at West Point were now compelled to apply their lessons in strategy and tactics against their old classmates; career soldiers who had first tasted battle together in the Mexican War would find their old comrades-

Fresh-faced Confederate militiamen anticipate their baptism of fire. Outnumbered by more than two to one, the million volunteers who took up arms for the Southern states drew strength from the fact that they were fighting to defend their homes and families.

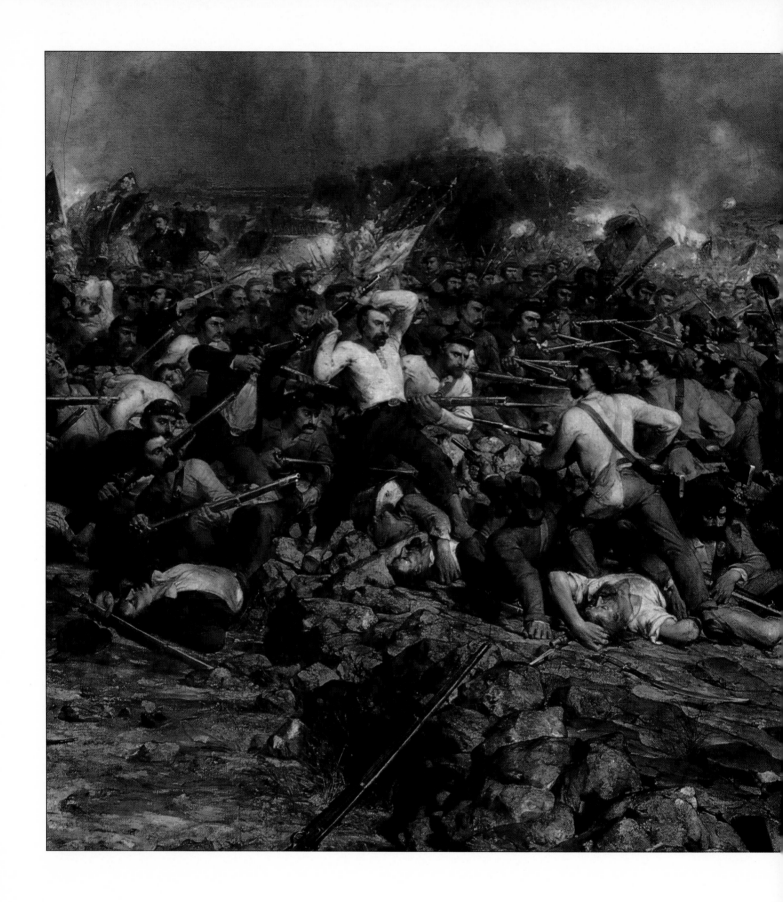

in-arms at the opposite end of their gunsights. Both sides were forced to rely heavily on hastily trained volunteers.

On the Union side, small-town militias were joined by newly formed urban regiments, some of which were composed entirely of immigrants, who brought with them the martial customs and traditions of their homelands. There were all-Irish and all-German units, as well as the kilted Highlanders who manned an all-Scottish regiment from New York. The Confederacy had assembled a fighting force of 60,000 volunteers by the time Fort Sumter was taken, but their training and resources varied widely: Seasoned army veterans marched alongside mountain boys armed with bowie knives and the rifles they used for shooting squirrels. Those soldiers possessing their own horses brought them along, to serve as cavalry mounts or to pull the artillery wagons. Many sons of the gentry were accompanied by their personal slaves, to cook their meals and keep their kits well cleaned and polished.

The Southerners believed passionately that they were fighting to maintain a principle and to protect a way of life, but in terms of supplies and armaments, they entered the war at a tremendous disadvantage. In 1860, the North manufactured 97 percent of all arms and munitions, and the vast majority of all textiles, boots, and shoes; the North was also far better endowed with an infrastructure of railways, paved roads, and canals, and with the industrial technology to adapt and extend this transportation network. In order to compensate for these shortfalls, Confederate leaders launched factory-building programs and traveled abroad to buy munitions and supplies. The South hoped to gain considerable support from the government of Great Britain: If the chaos of war prevented cotton from reaching the textile mills of England, the British economy would be shaken to its very foundation. James Bulloch, who took on the responsibility for converting civilian ships for combat use, persuaded British shipyards to fit out new vessels for the infant navy of the Confederacy.

While both sides worked to put their economies on a wartime footing, the generals devised their strategies. The Northern commander, General Winfield Scott, espoused the so-called anaconda approach—defeat by strangulation. Instead of invading the South and wreaking havoc that would later take enormous amounts of federal money to repair, Scott proposed to cut off access to the region by water. A blockade of warships would prevent European supply ships from landing along its Atlantic coast, while a cordon of gunboats and troops on the Mississippi River would besiege the Confederacy on its western flank. Northern politicians and the Northern public alike,

In this detail from a painting by Peter Frederick Rothermel of the Battle of Gettysburg, fought in Pennsylvania in July 1863, a Union soldier wields his musket as a club against the fixed bayonets of advancing Confederate troops. After three terrible days of fighting, more than 50,000 men were missing, wounded, or dead *(inset)*. The Union's victory ended the Confederacy's last attempt to invade the North. At the dedication of a cemetery on the battlefield that November, Lincoln vowed "that these dead shall not have died in vain—that this nation, under God, shall have a new birth of freedom."

143

The shells of burned-out warehouses stand like tombstones in Richmond, Virginia, the capital of the Confederacy, after the occupation of the city by Union forces on April 3, 1865. Two days later, as Lincoln walked the debris-littered streets, he was surrounded by crowds of joyous ex-slaves exulting in their freedom.

however, demanded more aggressive action: They wanted a swift invasion and suppression of the rebellious South.

The Confederate command developed an approach that Jefferson Davis called "offensive-defensive." They hoped to pull together their scattered forces to fight off any enemy incursions, while at the same time launching an invasion that would put the North on the defensive. But for any strategy to be effective, they needed to persuade states that lay on the border between North and South to join their cause.

The states of Maryland, Missouri, and Kentucky all had strong cultural and historical links with the South, but they had economic interests that militated against secession. Maryland, strategically important as a corridor for Union troops heading southward, was in any case home to many pro-Unionists, who realized that their prosperity depended on communications links with the North; nevertheless, approximately one-third of the white Marylanders who fought in the conflict did so on the rebel side. In Missouri, a pro-Southern faction set up its own legislature, but the secessionists were soon driven out of the state, and the majority of white Missourians fought in the Union army. Kentucky, bordered by three slave states and three free states, struggled to maintain a precarious neutrality, even offering to mediate between the combatants. Before the end of the year, however, Kentucky would become a battleground, occupied by both armies. The state legislature remained pro-Union, while the governor and other politicians broke off to form a provisional government that was admitted to the Confederacy.

The war of words was soon over. The first decisive military engagement came in July 1861, three months after the attack on Fort Sumter, at the battle in Virginia that the Confederates called Manassas and the Union named Bull Run. Many Northerners believed that their army had only to march into Virginia—which, even though it housed the Confederate capital, Richmond, was torn by dissension—and the ragtag rebel army would be trounced. Such optimists were now shocked out of their complacency. The Southerners held out against repeated Union assaults; and when the Northern forces grew weary, and no reinforcements were forthcoming, they were overwhelmed by a fierce counterattack. Confederate troops, uttering for the first time the bloodcurdling cry that would become known as the rebel yell, turned on their attackers, forced them into a panic-stricken retreat, and took more than 1,200 prisoners of war.

By the standards of later Civil War battles, the numbers of both combatants and

In a photograph taken eleven days after he had surrendered to the Union general Ulysses S. Grant, Robert E. Lee maintains the dignity and decorum that won him widespread respect. Opposed to both slavery and secession, he nevertheless remained loyal to his family background and became the Confederacy's most successful commander. Returned to civilian life, he encouraged his fellow Southerners to repair the damages of war in a spirit of reconciliation.

casualties were small, but the boost to Southern morale was enormous. From Virginia to Alabama, newspaper editors rhapsodized over the victory, urged the Confederate forces to lay waste to the Northern cities, and declared the North itself a spent force.

Cooler heads prevailed in the North. Confidence was shaken, but not destroyed. Lincoln ordered the enlistment of one million troops, enrolled for a three-year term of service. From farms and factory towns, volunteers poured in. The war to defeat the South became a crusade.

Northern manufacturers and financiers redoubled their efforts, and a barrage of patriotic advertisements persuaded individuals and institutions to buy war bonds, which would ultimately provide the government with two-thirds of the revenue needed for the war effort. As men departed for the front lines, employers coped with the labor shortage by investing in new forms of mechanized technology. Inflation, which had been troubling the economy even before the war began, continued to disrupt it: Workers complained that their wages were not keeping up with the spiraling cost of living, and the noise of the war machine in full swing was not successful in drowning out the sounds of industrial unrest that would lead to a wave of labor strikes before hostilities were over.

The economy of the South was in a far more precarious position. Much of the Confederacy's wealth was in the form of frozen assets, such as land and slaves. When war broke out, Southerners had in their hands only about one-tenth of the currency in circulation, and most Southern planters were deeply in debt to Northern bankers. Moreover, the Confederacy had no system for collecting taxes, and a population— previously only lightly taxed—that would have strongly resisted any levy. As in the North, war bonds were issued and vigorously promoted; those subscribers who had no ready cash were invited to make a financial pledge against the sale of future crops. In the end, more funds were pledged than paid, and the Confederacy was able to raise considerably less than half of its funds in this manner. As inflation soared, the value of the Confederate dollar seemed to grow smaller from day to day; by the time the war ended, it would be worth only one percent of its original value. The poorest segments of the white population were the hardest hit, and although they had been the most enthusiastic of the secessionists, they were the first to grow disenchanted with the Confederacy's cause.

The economy was further squeezed by the Northern embargoes on its exports, and

Under Citadel Rock in Wyoming Territory, a locomotive of the Union Pacific line advances across a newly constructed bridge over a snow-covered riverbed. The completion of a rail link between Nebraska and California in 1869 spurred the economic development of the West, reducing the cost of freighting agricultural produce and speeding its delivery. Wages for the laborers who laid the tracks were transported in strongboxes *(inset)* on the stagecoaches of the Wells Fargo company, founded in 1852.

by a naval blockade that was intended to keep Southern cotton, sugarcane, and other crops from reaching the European marketplace. To thwart the blockade, the Confederacy established a fleet of successful blockade runners, manned by daring Southerners and British soldiers of fortune, who shipped cotton to England and filled their holds with arms and ammunition on the westward voyage. "Hunting, pigsticking, steeplechasing, big-game hunting, polo—I have done a little of each," declared one English adventurer, "and all have their thrilling moments, but none can approach running a blockade!"

In the winter of 1862, the war took to the water. On the Atlantic coast, the Union navy hunted down vessels attempting to break the blockade. Inland, armored river craft clashed on the great waterways that ran down into the western part of the Confederacy. Along the Tennessee, Cumberland, and Mississippi rivers, the Union army and navy pressed deep into Confederate territory, challenged at every turn by rebel forces manning the forts along the banks. On this western front, the Union was heartened by a campaign that culminated in the blood-soaked victory of the battle of Shiloh at Pittsburg Landing, Tennessee, where 20,000 men from both sides were killed or wounded in two days of bitter fighting in cold and wet conditions. A few days later, Northern forces captured New Orleans, the Mississippi River's vital outlet to the sea and the South's most important port.

But the militant South, its troops now battle-hardened and its war machine functioning with greater efficiency, was unbowed. The summer and autumn of 1862 saw unequaled butchery, especially on the northern front; and in September, the Confederate Army of Northern Virginia met the Union Army of the Potomac in the battle that Southerners named Sharpsburg and the North called Antietam. Confederate troops, led by General Robert E. Lee, had entered Union territory and held a position in the state of Maryland perilously close to the national capital at Washington, D.C. To the commander of the Northern forces, General George B. McClellan, Lincoln's orders could not have been more simple: "Destroy the rebel army!"

Although McClellan did not succeed—indeed, his critics claimed that, through a lack of decisive action at the strategic moment, he did not so much win Antietam as allow his battered opponents to lose it—he presided over a scene of unprecedented destruction. It was later estimated that twice as many casualties were counted in Antietam in a single day as were suffered by the military forces of the United States cumulatively in the War of 1812, the Mexican War, and the Spanish-American War of 1898. Even as the smoke cleared and the stench of blood and rotting flesh was carried from the battlefield, both sides knew the war had reached a turning point.

Five days after Antietam, Lincoln issued his most decisive moral challenge to the Confederacy. Just a month before, he had argued that "My paramount object in this struggle is to save the Union, and is not either to save or to destroy slavery." Now, however, he sensed that only by adding to this primary goal the abolition of slavery could a decisive victory be won. On September 22, he issued a preliminary emancipation proclamation, promising to free all slaves

THE PLAINS INDIANS: A HERITAGE DESTROYED

The gulf between the cultures of the Indians and the white settlers in the West of America rendered peaceful coexistence well-nigh impossible. On the vast prairies stretching from the Mississippi to the Rocky Mountains and south to Mexico, the Indians lived as nomadic hunters; their homes were made of buffalo hide, as in the Arapaho camp in southwest Oklahoma shown below. The whites were farmers and town dwellers, who seized the Indians' land for their settlements.

The U.S. government sought to pen up the Indians on reservations where, unable to hunt the migrating herds of buffalo, they became dependent on handouts of beef. The Indians resisted, using newly acquired firearms and swift horses—introduced from Spanish Mexico in the seventeenth century—to fight an effective guerrilla war. At Little Bighorn in Montana Territory in 1876, Sioux warriors wiped out an entire force of more than 200 soldiers led by Lieutenant Colonel George Armstrong Custer.

In the 1880s, many tribes adopted a religion called Ghost Dance that promised a regenerated world and resurrection. But in 1890, U.S. troops, enforcing a ban on the faith, killed 200 unarmed Indians, mostly women and children, at Wounded Knee Creek in South Dakota. Against guns and steel, even the ancestors were powerless.

Painted with the images of a mystic vision, this buckskin shirt was worn by an Arapaho adherent of the Ghost Dance religion. Indians believed such shirts made them immune to the white man's bullets.

within the territory under Confederate control unless the rebel states returned to the Union. This was followed by a final proclamation on January 1, 1863, which declared the slaves of the South to be free—as soon as the Union forces could enter rebel territory to break their chains.

By turning a civil war into a war of liberation, Lincoln gained a number of political and military advantages. The possibility that the British government—which had passed its own antislavery laws in 1833—might intervene on behalf of the South—was ended. Northern morale was stiffened, and for many Southerners, continuing the struggle now seemed futile. The proclamation encouraged large numbers of slaves to run away from their masters, and it opened up the Union forces to black recruits.

Although the Union navy had maintained its tradition of enlisting men of any race, the Union army had so far not recruited any members of the small population of free blacks living in Northern cities. Even now, it would take a considerable struggle on the part of the 130,000 black troops to gain parity in pay. After milder means had failed, black regiments launched a pay strike; they accepted no salary payments for nearly two years, until the president agreed to end the discrepancy. Lincoln had little choice: Their participation was vital to the war effort, and in many clashes, black regiments had borne the brunt of the casualties. In the course of the war, one in three black enlisted men was killed or wounded—twice the loss rate for their white comrades-in-arms.

As the body count mounted, the South suffered two more devastating blows: In the summer of 1863, another Confederate incursion into the North ended in a shattering defeat at Gettysburg, Pennsylvania, and on the western front, the Confederate stronghold of Vicksburg, Mississippi, was forced to surrender after a prolonged and punishing siege. Contemporary observers remarked that the South had, in effect, lost the war, but the North had not yet won it.

Early in 1864, Lincoln appointed General Ulysses S. Grant, lauded for his successful siege of Vicksburg, as supreme commander of the Union forces. As Grant launched into an aggressive campaign against Robert E. Lee's Virginia armies, his fellow general, William Sherman, led an invasion force that hammered its way through Tennessee and Georgia, destroying the roads and railway track that served as vital Confederate supply lines. In September, he captured the city of Atlanta, whose inhabitants fled in panic.

For both the war-weary North and the hungry South, mourning the failure of its hopes, the taking of Atlanta signaled the beginning of the end. At the outset of 1865, Jefferson Davis began discreet exploratory discussions with Northern envoys to consider terms for a possible peace. On certain issues, Lincoln was adamant: National authority had to be restored immediately to the federal government in Washington; there could be no compromise on the question of slavery; no merely temporary truce was acceptable; and all anti-Union forces must immediately be disbanded and sent home. Davis had hoped for more flexible negotiations, and the war dragged on until the spring, when General Lee regretfully advised that the besieged Confederate capital at Richmond should be evacuated. On April 9, with his supply lines cut off and rations running out, Lee surrendered to Grant at Appomattox Court House, seventy-five miles west of Richmond.

On the streets of the Northern cities, men and women danced, sang, prayed, and wept for joy. Just five days after Lee's surrender, however, these festivities were brought to a sudden end. For several weeks, an embittered Southern sympathizer, the actor John Wilkes Booth, had been organizing a murderous conspiracy. On the evening of April 14, during a performance at Ford's Theater in Washington, Booth assassinated President Lincoln.

A shocked nation, forcibly reunited, counted the costs of the conflict: hundreds of thousands of men dead on both sides, farms and plantations laid waste, roads and railways in ruins, and the population in many districts on the brink of starvation. The policies of reconstruction were anxiously and acrimoniously debated. Should the federal government treat the shattered South as a conquered country, deserving due punishment for having dared to rebel, or welcome it back into the Union and pour in resources to heal its wounds? When should the military governors of the ex-Confederate states hand back control to the civil powers? Should former Confederate leaders be allowed to hold public office? And what was to become of the former slaves, now forced to fend for themselves in a hostile world?

The plight of the freed slaves, who in theory had more to gain from the victory of the North than anyone, was the most pressing problem. The abolitionist leader Frederick Douglass, himself a former slave who had fled to freedom, would later describe their misery:

The world has never seen any people turned loose to such destitution as were the four million slaves of the South. . . . They were free! Free to

Buffalo carcasses testify to the lethal efficiency of the rifle aslant a horse's saddle. Hunters also shot the animals from special excursion trains, using weapons equipped with telescopic sights that could kill at a range of 550 yards. Herds of as many as 15 million in the 1860s were reduced to just a few hundred head by the end of the century. As the territory roamed by buffalo steadily diminished, so too did that inhabited by America's Indians, who lived on the animals' meat and made tents and blankets from their hides.

Seconds after the firing of a single rifle shot at noon on September 16, 1893, eager settlers race to stake their claims to free land. For this last of a series of "land rushes," more than 100,000 pioneers and immigrants had arrived in Oklahoma Territory to take their chances in the stampede for 6.5 million acres of territory purchased by the government from the Cherokee Indians. Each would-be farmer was allowed to claim 160 acres on the condition that he cultivate the land and live on it for at least five years.

hunger, free to the pitiless wrath of enraged masters. . . . Free, without roofs to cover them, or bread to eat, or land to cultivate.

Congress took swift action. New laws and constitutional amendments were passed that gave black male Americans full citizenship, made the federal government responsible for protecting individual civil rights, reconstructed the state governments, and established a Freedmen's Bureau to help liberated slaves survive and adjust to their altered circumstances.

These achievements were hard won and were often short-lived, however. The liberal members in the House of Representatives and the Senate found themselves pitted against a new president, Andrew Johnson, who made no secret of his racial prejudices. "This is a country for white men," he declared, "and, by God, so long as I am president, it shall be a government for white men." Johnson's Congressional

opponents, roused to fury by his obstructions, brought a case for his impeachment. The president was placed on trial, with the Senate serving as jury, but the last-minute qualms of seven of the senators prevented them from casting the votes that were required to remove Johnson from office.

The conservative citizens of the conquered South were also unwilling to accept the sweeping social changes thrust upon them. They looked with contempt upon the scalawags, fellow Southerners who had originally opposed secession from the Union, and who now emerged to play their part in the restructuring of their society. And they loathed even more the Northerners who now poured into the region as government officials, agents of business firms and financial institutions, teachers, and technicians. Known as carpetbaggers, from the bags containing all the possessions with which they arrived, some of these newcomers were genuine idealists, impelled by a spirit of missionary zeal to help build the new South; many more were economic opportunists, grasping the chance to make themselves an easy fortune in a fast-moving but still chaotic environment. Never before had the South seen so much money changing hands, as public officials and private entrepreneurs launched into public-works projects, railroad construction, and the creation of new schools for a region previously lacking any form of state education.

Because the South was still dependent on its agriculture, there was a pressing need for labor to plant and harvest the staple crops. The obvious source was the large ex-slave population, but the Southern farmers and planters found themselves caught in a vicious circle: Until the crops were harvested, they would have no cash to pay wages, but if no laborers worked the land, there would be no crop.

The solution devised by planters in many areas was to divide up their land into tenant farms that the ex-slaves could work for themselves, a system known as sharecropping. But the new tenants had no resources other than their labor, so the landlord had to supply the ill-furnished shacks they lived in, as well as the tools needed to work the land. The sum that a sharecropper owed for these necessities, which were rented on credit, often equaled or exceeded the payment he received for his crops, forcing him into perpetual debt.

In many areas the Freedmen's Bureau initiated land-distribution programs, giving rise to a widespread rumor that each emancipated household would be granted "forty acres and a mule." But these projects were usually based on short-term loans rather than outright gifts of land or livestock, and few recipients had the resources to exercise the option to purchase their property once the term of the loan was up.

The ex-slaves who had the best chances of prosperity were those who had managed to learn a trade, and the ones who had slipped away through the hidden trails and safe houses of the Underground Railroad—a clandestine network of slaves, free blacks, and a few white abolitionists—to a new life in the North. Even before the war began, some 500,000 black people had lived outside the slavery system. A privileged few had studied medicine, law, or theology, and they now lived in small enclaves of black professionals and businessmen in New York, Cincinnati, and even in the South itself—notably in Charleston and New Orleans—where the wealthiest among them had themselves become slave owners.

The white supremacists who dominated Southern society were united in their determination to deny full citizenship to their black neighbors. By the mid-1870s, federal involvement in the postwar Reconstruction programs was effectively over, and early initiatives to allow black men to vote or hold public office were a thing of

Members of a pioneer family don their Sunday best for a photograph on their homestead in western Kansas. Because there were no trees on the plains, houses were made of dried sod, and buffalo dung was used for fuel. The rich soil supported abundant crops of wheat and other cereals, but many farmers were ruined by drought, floods, blizzards, or prairie fires.

the past. Counties and states introduced restrictive legislation that curtailed the civil rights of the black population. Secret racist organizations such as the Ku Klux Klan arose to initiate a reign of terror, lynching so-called troublemakers, burning houses, and killing livestock, to ensure that black people did not protest, or make any unwelcome demands for justice.

Even while the Civil War had raged in the East, America's rush to conquer and tame its vast transcontinental territory continued. And in the postwar years, as legislators and entrepreneurs applied all their energies to setting the United States back on course to prosperity, the newly freed slaves of the South were not the only nonwhites to be cast aside by the juggernaut of social and economic change that now rolled over the entire nation.

During the course of the Civil War, Congress had taken advantage of the absence of Southern legislators—who had in general strongly opposed federal expenditure on railroad projects in the West—to vote into law the Pacific Railroad Act of 1862. Federal lands and funds were granted to a consortium of investors to assist the construction of a rail link between Omaha, Nebraska, and San Francisco Bay. In 1863, a work force that was made up mainly of imported Chinese laborers had begun to lay the Central Pacific lines running eastward from Sacramento, California, while Irish immigrants—later joined by demobilized soldiers—assembled the Union Pacific tracks heading westward. On May 10, 1869, the two lines met at Promontory Point, Utah, and were hammered together, to the accompaniment of ringing bells and cannon fire, with a ceremonial golden spike.

The proximity of the railroad could make or break a community, and much behind-the-scenes jockeying took place among rail companies, land speculators, and politicians over proposed new routes. The towns of the Pacific Coast—Portland, San Francisco, Seattle—would soon grow into self-sufficient cities, linked to the markets, banks, and stock exchanges of the East by telegraph wires and metal rails. The laborious journeys of settlers heading west had been simplified, and the populations of many western states now soared. The number of inhabitants in Kansas and Nebraska, for example, nearly tripled between 1870 and 1880.

The Homestead Act, another piece of wartime legislation, had established land grants to foster new settlement. An allocation of 160 acres of federal land was available free of charge to any applicant, male or female, who was prepared to occupy, improve, and farm it, and after five years' residence, the homesteader became the owner of the land. By the end of the century, 500,000 families would take up the offer, turning 80 million acres of virgin territory into farms.

But as this new American population made a home for itself in the West, an older one was displaced and driven out. The native American tribes, who had been progressively pent up in smaller and smaller tracts of territory, now found that a fresh influx of white settlers cast covetous eyes on their remaining pastures and hunting grounds. Long-standing treaties were torn up by the authorities, especially when the lands concerned ran alongside the routes of new railroads, and tribes were forced to sell or surrender their property in exchange for dubious promises in which the Indians soon lost all faith. "The white man made us many promises," recalled Chief Red Cloud of the Sioux, "more than I can remember, but they never kept but one; they promised to take our land, and they took it."

Tribal leaders met in councils, and pondered how to counter the invasion. Government proposals to confine the tribes to reservations were met with strong resistance. Satanta, of the Kiowa, made an eloquent stand against the white invaders: "I have heard that you want to settle us on a reservation. I don't want to settle. I love

In a painting by Frederic Remington, a dismounted cowboy prepares to raise the wooden poles that form a gate in a barbed-wire fence. Invented in 1874 by Joseph Glidden, barbed wire provided a cheap means for homesteaders to protect their crops from the grazing of cattle. The cowboys who controlled the free-ranging herds were eventually forced to enclose their own land and settle down as ranchers.

to roam over the prairies. There I feel free and happy, but when I settle down I pale and die." But Satanta was not permitted to follow the traditions of his forebears. He was confined to a prison hospital in Texas, and in 1878, Satanta threw himself to his death from a high window.

The wars of resistance continued sporadically throughout the 1870s and 1880s, until the last great struggle of the Apache tribes in the southwest, led by Geronimo, was finally lost. And what the artillery of the U.S. Army and the harassment by ranchers and railroaders did not achieve, the bullets of white hunters completed. The vast herds of buffalo—from which the Indians derived hides for shelter and clothing as well as food—were virtually exterminated, and the tribes were starved into submitting to the white man's will.

Throughout the North and West, large towns were now drawing into themselves all the energy and wealth of the hinterland, and finance capital—the most important raw material of the age—was being generated for further investment. With the essential grid of transport and communications networks laid down, America was ready to transform the process of territorial expansion into that of economic growth. In pursuit of ever higher profits, the nation's entrepreneurs would prove themselves as ruthless and, ultimately, as successful as the land pioneers they succeeded.

As the populations of the towns were swollen both by ambitious migrants from the countryside and foreign-born immigrants, financiers and businessmen provided funds for the infrastructure needed to match this increase. Public works were initiated on an unprecedented scale, schools and hospitals erected, sewer systems laid down, water supplies improved. Investment opportunities multiplied. Political bosses became skilled in courting speculators and trading favors to get work done, and done fast, even if ethics and legality were sometimes sidestepped in the process.

The public was appalled but intrigued by this new breed of urban manipulator. The year 1871 saw the exposure of a New Yorker named William Tweed, a jovial tyrant who had bought the loyalty of Irish immigrants in his district through acts of godfatherly benevolence, and who could deliver their votes by the ballot boxful at election time. "Boss" Tweed had also forged a network of corrupt cronies, known as the Tweed Ring. Its membership included building contractors who knew how to pad an estimate and split a fee, public officials with lucrative projects to bestow, police inspectors willing to turn a blind eye to violations, and heavy-handed henchmen who could quell all opposition.

Tweed would fall, but his tribe was legion, and in metropolitan areas from Boston to Chicago to the new boom towns farther west, the pattern repeated itself. A new boss would rise to power, grow fat and complacent, and then be deposed by a reform administration advertising itself as a "new broom" to sweep city politics clean. The intricacies of governing ever-larger urban centers, however, would quickly prove too much for the idealistic novices, and other bosses—more discreet, at first, than their predecessors—would soon emerge to take control again.

Wheeling and dealing in their petty kingdoms, each new ring of city bosses and developers soon learned how to cul-

Traders, shoppers, delivery boys, carts, and carriages congest New York City's Mulberry Street in 1895. During the second half of the nineteenth century, a tide of immigrants flooded into the United States at the rate of around 500,000 per year, providing cheap labor for industries in the North and boosting agricultural settlement in the West. In some areas of Manhattan Island, the chief port of entry on the east coast, the population density in 1890 exceeded 900 people per acre. Many Irish, Italian, Greek, Polish, and Russian newcomers clustered together in neighborhoods that became microcosms of their homelands, with shops and newspapers functioning in their native languages.

A solitary observer ponders the industrial landscape of the Homestead Steel Works near Pittsburgh, Pennsylvania, the largest in America. Founded by the Scottish-born Andrew Carnegie, this plant had its own railroad and steamships to bring in supplies of coal and iron ore; it employed immigrant laborers who worked twelve hours a day, seven days a week. The defeat of a five-month strike in 1892 was effective in destroying the union movement in the steel industry for a generation. In 1901, Carnegie sold his companies to the United States Steel Corporation and gave away most of his fortune to establish colleges, schools, and a pension fund for his former workers.

tivate allies in high places and to squeeze out competition. But a system controlled by a small and intimate network of financial magnates and industrialists was more vulnerable than they realized, and in the 1870s, the bosses faced new challenges to their power.

The crash of financier Jay Cooke's massive banking firm in 1873 triggered a national depression, caused the failure of many large and small businesses, and led to a wave of bitter strikes. Labor unions rose up to defend the livelihood of their members; in the South and West, farmers formed similar alliances to foster their collective interests. In the cities, crusading journalists exposed the exploitation of the poor by unscrupulous slum landlords and large-scale employers alike.

In 1877, the United States had its first taste of industrial action on a national scale. The Baltimore and Ohio railroad line, pleading economic necessity, made repeated cuts in its employees' wages. Wildcat strikes spread along the rail lines with the speed of an express train, bringing bloodshed in their wake. In Philadelphia, Pittsburgh, Chicago, and San Francisco, vigilantes hired by the rail company attacked striking workers, mobs of ordinary citizens joined in on both sides, and looters took advantage of the violence in the streets. Federal troops were called in to quell the riots, and they dispersed the mobs. Jittery businessmen were reassured by this show of strength, convinced that the government was firmly on their side, but their relief was short-lived.

During a local strike in Chicago in 1886, a group of German-born anarchists organized a protest meeting and the city police force arrived to break up the gathering. A bomb suddenly exploded, killing one man and wounding six others. The police moved in, and at least seven members of the crowd died under the blows of their night sticks. Although no bomber was identified, eight anarchists were rounded up, subjected to kangaroo-court trials, and condemned to death. A vocal law-and-order lobby claimed that the nation's peace and prosperity were being threatened by subversive immigrant agitators and rebellious workers. Judges, generally drawn from the affluent sectors of society, were impelled to greater severity in their treatment of crimes against property and challenges to the established order.

A growing portion of the electorate now questioned the premise that financial might makes right. As economic power appeared to concentrate ever more intensely in the hands of a small group of capitalists, Congress responded to public pressure by drafting legislation to curb the worst price-fixing and competition-squeezing excesses of big-business monopolies, popularly known as the "trusts." In practice, however, this law was enforced more vigorously against labor unions than against employers. A new political party, the Populists, enjoyed a brief period of success in the 1890s, on a platform criticizing the country's large corporations and their systems of providing financial credit and distributing goods.

As the economy continued to move through cycles of boom and bust, divisions between workers and their bosses grew ever wider. An 1893 depression wreaked havoc. Many farming regions were ravaged by drought, insect plagues, and dust storms, and those farmers who managed to harvest their crops found themselves faced with a sudden deflation in the price of grain. One in four of the unskilled laborers in the cities was thrown out of work. In 1894, a reformer named Jacob Coxey

American troops at Tampa, Florida, prepare for embarkation to Cuba in 1898. Siding with Cuban revolutionaries who sought independence from Spain, American forces seized Santiago and defeated a Spanish fleet in the Philippines. At the end of the four-month war, Spain ceded Puerto Rico, Guam, and the Philippines to the United States, which now appeared on the world stage in the unaccustomed role of an imperial power.

led several thousand unemployed workers from the North and West in a march on Washington, describing the action as a "petition in boots" addressed to an apparently indifferent government. The march was peaceful but the atmosphere was tense: Coxey's Army was met at every stopping place by armed militiamen and local vigilantes. It was finally dispersed.

In that same year, the workers at the Pullman Company, manufacturers of railroad cars, launched a strike against their management. To support the strikers, the railroad union organized a boycott of all Pullman cars currently running on the railroads, and the national rail system seemed about to grind to a halt. Overriding the opposition of the reform-minded governor of Illinois, who did not wish to see his national guard troops used for strikebreaking, the United States attorney general sent federal troops into the state.

By such actions, capitalists were reassured that the federal government was on their side. Yet they recognized that a nation of such massive size and complexity would inevitably be subject to legislation affecting commerce and industry. To further their interests they became increasingly skilled in manipulating the political system to their own advantage, throwing their considerable financial weight behind candidates known to be sympathetic. Railroad magnate Collis P. Huntington was typical in his approach. Writing to a business associate after a meeting with the governor of New Mexico, Huntington reported: "I saw Axtell, and he said he thought that if we would send him such a bill as we wanted to have passed into a law, he could get it passed with very little money."

Yet even those citizens made uneasy by the methods of big business could not fail to be impressed by its energy and achievements. For a majority of the population, lives had been made easier and prosperity enhanced. While much wealth had accumulated in the hands of the nation's new aristocracy of millionaires, large amounts of capital had also been invested in public institutions. Colleges and universities, funded by private benefactors as well as by local and federal government grants, were becoming accessible to all. Affluence was in reach of even the poorest foreign immigrants, for whom education offered opportunities to break out of their inward-looking urban communities.

The nation's entrepreneurs had proved their worth: They had spanned the continent with rail and telegraph lines, mined the minerals under its surface, and powered the industries that were a match for any in the developed world. And now that the great empty spaces were conquered and settled, the industrialists and their bankers began to look to new horizons. The United States was about to become a player on an even larger stage.

Across the Pacific Ocean, new markets beckoned. European nations were jockeying for commercial and political influence in the newly opened port cities of China, and the United States was determined not to be left out of this bonanza. In 1898, the acquisition of the Hawaiian Islands, in mid-Pacific, provided a useful base of operations on the vital route between California and the Orient. Closer to home, the nation's leaders began to realize the strategic and economic importance of their Caribbean neighbors,

Rising more than 300 feet high in New York Harbor, the Statue of Liberty presides over scenes of popular rejoicing at its unveiling in October 1886. A gift to America from the people of France, the statue was constructed of copper sheets over a giant steel framework, then disassembled and shipped across the Atlantic. To millions of immigrants from Europe who continued to enter America in the early years of the twentieth century, it was their first sight of the country that had become the world's most powerful nation and to which their hopes for a better life were entrusted.

especially when they considered the possibility of a canal across the Isthmus of Panama, linking the Atlantic and Pacific oceans.

To further and protect its overseas interests, the government poured fresh resources into its naval forces. Before the 1880s, the United States Navy was smaller than those of many Latin American republics; by the end of the century, it was the third largest in the world. Bolstered by new ships and the confidence that went with them, the Republic in 1898 entered upon its first major overseas military adventure, launching into a war against the decaying imperial power of Spain.

Victory, achieved with a speed that surprised even the most optimistic supporters of the action, brought many prizes: the Philippine Islands and Guam in the Pacific, Puerto Rico in the Caribbean, and considerable influence over the fledgling republic of Cuba, whose own bid for independence had been the apparent inspiration for the war with Spain. Throughout the Americas, the United States was now the dominant political and economic power; with her strategic foothold in the Pacific, she was also well placed to take advantage of any mercantile gold rush in the Far East.

Some citizens recoiled from the notion that the United States, itself the child of rebellion against colonial rule, should now be in the position of an imperial power, with its flag and its warships maintaining a presence on territory far from home. But for others it was the occasion of celebration. "The power that rules the Pacific," exulted Senator Albert Beveridge, "is the power that rules the world. And, with the Philippines, that power is, and will for ever be, the American republic. The trade of the world must and shall be ours."

For Beveridge and for many of his compatriots, the drive to look outward was the logical extension of the spirit of Manifest Destiny that had driven Americans across the prairies, mountains, and deserts. Half a century of turbulent change had given them confidence and courage; they had weathered a storm that had threatened to tear their republic to shreds, had seen democratic institutions continue to work even in the midst of this chaos, and had observed that enterprise could reap magnificent rewards. They were motivated not just by commercial opportunism, but by a conviction that they had devised the best of all possible political and economic systems, which should now be bestowed upon a waiting world.

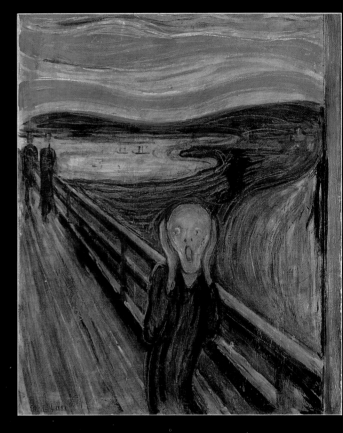

"The prevalent feeling," wrote the Hungarian-born Jewish author Max Nordau in the 1890s, "is of imminent perdition and extinction."

To many of the citizens of Europe who gathered in public squares on December 31, 1899, to celebrate the end of a century of unprecedented change, such sentiments were heresy. In terms of health, longevity, and material comfort, the quality of their lives had vastly improved; and the wealth and power generated by technological advances had enabled Europe to dominate all other civilizations as never before. But on the fringes of the crowds there were awkward loners. They included, in the words of the German philosopher Friedrich Nietzsche, who died in 1900, "the bravest spirits who must be the conscience of the modern soul, and as such must be its consciousness, concentrating all the disease, poison, and danger that only modern times could have produced." The mood was intensely expressed in *The Cry (right),* by the Norwegian painter Edvard Munch in 1893, and in the troubled visions of the artists whose work appears on the following pages.

The anxieties that surfaced in Europe in the 1890s were most sharply focused in the city of Vienna, dubbed by the writer Karl Kraus "the experimental station for the end of the world." In this ornate capital of the decaying Austro-Hungarian Empire, rife with anti-Semitism, tensions produced by economic hardship and an aggressive nationalism were barely concealed by a veneer of gentility and rigid etiquette. The atmosphere was described by the novelist Stefan Zweig as "sticky, perfumed, sultry, unhealthy. . . . Everywhere the suppressed sought byways, loopholes, and detours."

Such outlets—which included fantasy, hysteria, and madness—were explored by the psychiatrist Sigmund Freud, the most influential of a gifted generation of Jewish artists and intellectuals. Freud's psychoanalysis of "the discomfort of civilization," and his theories about the unconscious instincts that motivate behavior, disclosed a

Cornfield with Crows (1890) exemplifies the Dutch painter Vincent van Gogh's dictum that "real artists paint things not as they are, but as they feel them." Just weeks after completing this picture in Auvers-sur-Oise in northern France, van Gogh committed suicide.

Masklike, parodic faces, half-comic and half-frightening, discomfort the viewer in the Belgian artist James Ensor's *Intrigue* (1890).

In *The Yellow Christ* (1889), Paul Gauguin imbued the paramount Christian icon—modeled on a wooden statue in a chapel near Pont-Aven in France—with both realism and mystery by setting it against the daily life of the Breton countryside.

malaise that all the century's achievements in medicine and education were powerless to alleviate. Freud's theories made it harder than ever to keep faith with the mainspring of the liberal politics of the first half of the century—the belief in the power of human reason to effect social improvement.

Throughout Europe, other dogmas were also crumbling. The collapse of the Berlin and Frankfurt stock exchanges on May 9, 1873—a date that became known as Black Friday—had inaugurated a severe economic depression whose effects were felt throughout Europe. Massive investment, prompted in part by gold discoveries in America and Australia in midcentury, had resulted in a growth of industrial capacity that was now no longer met by demand, and thousands were thrown out of work. Strikes and the increasing use of violence by extreme socialist movements dented the confident, expansionist assumptions of the middle class. Émile Zola's harshly realistic novels about the lives of the French working class and Charles Booth's seventeen-volume survey of the London poor focused attention on those whom progress and prosperity had bypassed. To many, such evidence appeared to lend weight to the political analysis of Karl Marx, who in the heyday of capitalism had prophesied its doom.

Traditional Christian beliefs had been challenged by Charles Darwin, who in *On the Origin of Species* (1859) suggested that man had come into the world as "a hairy quadruped, furnished with a tail and pointed ears," and that his present form was the result of millennia of evolution. Crudely applied to politics in the guise of Social Darwinism, Darwin's concept of the "survival of the fittest" appeared to justify aggressive foreign policies and to render futile all attempts to ameliorate social inequalities. Even the solidity of physical matter itself appeared to be dissolving, as scientists probing its consistency discovered that matter comprises minute, subatomic particles surrounded by space.

Responses to this crisis of confidence took various forms. The most extreme was analyzed by the pioneering French sociologist Émile Durkheim in his study *Suicide* (1897), which demonstrated how individuals might be affected by social disruption. The painter Paul Gauguin, convinced of the moral bankruptcy of Western society, fled France for the islands of the South Pacific in 1891, while the poet Arthur Rimbaud renounced his art at the age of nineteen and lived as a wanderer and gunrunner in the Middle East.

Many, as if sensing their release from old taboos, turned to straightforward amusement—for which the *fin-de-siècle* years provided abundant opportunities, either in the music halls and cabarets of Europe's capital cities, newly illuminated by gaslight or electricity, or in the more literary form of witty, satirical plays and magazines. In London, high society followed the lead of Queen Victoria's eldest son, the plump and raffish Albert Edward, who kept a string of mistresses and devoted his time to parties, gambling, shooting, yachting, and more parties. Those who fell foul of the law still had to pay the price: The dramatist Oscar Wilde was imprisoned for two years after the exposure of a homosexual affair, and a play by George Bernard Shaw about a barmaid in Waterloo Station who becomes a prostitute, written in 1894, was banned from the stage until 1925. But there was a scent of forbidden delights in the air, and an eagerness to test the limits of freedom.

Certainly for artists of all kinds, a loss of faith in social and aesthetic conventions alike proved as liberating as it was disturbing. The poet Stéphane Mallarmé forsook strict metrical forms and used language for its purely symbolical qualities. The composers Gustav Mahler and Arnold Schoenberg in Vienna and Claude Debussy in Paris experimented with new systems of harmony or musical structure. Beginning in the 1870s, a group of French painters, including Claude Monet and Auguste Renoir, pioneered a revolutionary style of painting, known as Impressionism, in which the artist's experience of his subject matter was directly transcribed onto the canvas in rapid brushstrokes of brilliant color.

Faithful to the dynamic and transient nature of human experience, Impressionist painting challenged the fixed rules of perspective that had governed Western art for five centuries, and it prepared the way for the more expressive, emotionally charged styles of the 1890s. The artists themselves were largely ignored or derided by the rest of society: Old habits die hard, and most people who shared in the material prosperity of the age were able to maintain, at least in public, a trust in their grandfathers' convictions. But the images of a mouth gaping in a silent scream of anguish, of black crows over windswept corn, of the spirit of war exulting over the naked bodies of the slain—were not just personal. Fleshing out a common disquiet, these paintings articulated a new and distinctly modern sensibility: anxious, uncertain, breasting the future with as much fear as hope.

In an 1882 lithograph, the French painter Odilon Redon tried to create a symbolic image that "raises the spirit into the realms of mystery, into the anxiety of the unresolved."

To the catalog accompanying the exhibition of Henri Rousseau's *War* in 1894, the self-taught artist added the commentary: "She passes in terrifying fashion leaving everywhere despair, tears, and ruin."

In this detail from *The Great Bathers* (1898-1905) by Paul Cézanne, figures and setting are fused in an arching design that reconciled the artist's determination to find new ways of transcribing nature with his continuing need for order and harmony.

INDIA

1850-1860	1860-1870
The Indian Mutiny breaks out at Meerut, northeast of Delhi, and spreads rapidly across northern and central India (1857). After the suppression of the Indian Mutiny in 1858, the British government takes over direct control of India from the East India Company.	British rule is consolidated by public works such as railroads and irrigation canals, whose construction is coordinated by the Indian Civil Service.

GERMANY

1850-1860	1860-1870
Helmuth von Moltke becomes Prussian chief of staff (1858) and begins to modernize the Prussian army.	William accedes as king of Prussia (1861). Otto von Bismarck is appointed prime minister of Prussia (1862). Prussia and Austria go to war with Denmark; victory in 1864 gives them joint control of the disputed provinces of Schleswig and Holstein. After defeating Austria at the Battle of Sadova (1866), Bismarck forms the North German Confederation, including all German states north of the Main River.

AFRICA

1850-1860	1860-1870
The Scottish missionary and explorer David Livingstone crosses Africa from west to east (1854-1856) and calls for increased commercial activity in the interests of Christianity and colonization. In West Africa, the French advance up the Senegal River (1854). The British take control of the island of Zanzibar off the east coast to combat the Arab slave trade (1856).	Diamonds are discovered in southern Africa (1866). The Suez Canal, linking the Egyptian port of Port Said on the Mediterranean coast to the Red Sea, is opened (1869).

AUSTRALIA

1850-1860	1860-1870
Victoria, South Australia, and Tasmania elect their first colonial legislatures (1850), following the example set by New South Wales in 1842. Gold is discovered in New South Wales and Victoria (1851), accelerating immigration to Australia. Troops storm a defensive stockade erected by goldminers at Eureka in Victoria, killing twenty-five (1854).	Robert O'Hara Burke and William John Wills complete the first overland crossing of Australia (1861), but they die of starvation on the return journey. The transportation of British convicts to Australia finally ceases (1868).

THE UNITED STATES

1850-1860	1860-1870
Violence erupts between proslavery and antislavery factions in Kansas (1855). The Supreme Court, in a ruling on the case of Dred Scott, decides that blacks are not entitled to the protection of the U.S. Constitution (1857). Antislavery militants attack a government arsenal at Harpers Ferry, Virginia (1859). Their leader, John Brown, is hanged for treason. Abraham Lincoln is elected president (1860). South Carolina and six other southern states declare their secession from the Union.	The Confederate States frame their own constitution (1861). The Civil War begins. After the Union victory at Antietam, Lincoln issues an emancipation proclamation, promising to free all slaves (1862). The last Confederate incursion into the North is defeated at Gettysburg (1863). Richmond, the Confederate capital, is taken; the South surrenders (1865). Lincoln is assassinated. The Union and Central Pacific railroad is completed, linking Nebraska to California (1869).

TimeFrame AD 1850-1900

1870-1880	1880-1890	1890-1900

Famine causes widespread loss of life in western and central India in 1896 and 1899.

Following a failure of the monsoon rains in 1876, famine claims several million lives in south India.

Queen Victoria is proclaimed empress of India (1876).

A group of mainly Hindu middle-class professionals forms the Indian National Congress (1885) and calls for more extensive employment of Indians in the administration.

The assassination of two British officials in 1897 signals the increasing use of violence by radical Indian nationalists.

Lord Curzon is appointed viceroy (1898).

German forces defeat the armies of Napoleon III of France (1870) and seize Paris. After Bismarck secures the alliance of the south German states, William is proclaimed emperor, or *Kaiser,* of the new German empire (1871).

The Berlin stock exchange crashes (1873), heralding a period of economic depression throughout Europe.

Bismarck establishes German protectorates in Africa (1883-1885).

Emperor William dies (1888); he is succeeded by his son Frederick, who dies three months later, and then by his grandson, William II.

After failing to secure the emperor's support for his plans to crush socialism, Bismarck resigns his post as German chancellor (1890).

Bismarck dies (1898).

The American journalist and explorer H. M. Stanley finds the ailing Livingstone at Ujiji on Lake Tanganyika (1871). In 1873, Livingstone dies.

Stanley discovers the source of the White Nile in Burundi (1874). Funded by Leopold II of Belgium, he founds trading posts along the Congo (1879).

The British invade the territory of the Ashanti in West Africa (1874).

In southern Africa, the British are defeated by Zulu warriors at the Battle of Isandhlwana (1879).

The British take control of the government of Egypt (1882). In 1885, a British garrison at Khartoum in the Sudan is massacred by the army of the Mahdi.

Following the Berlin Congress (1884), the Congo Free State is established under the rule of Leopold of Belgium. Germany declares protectorates in Togoland, the Cameroons, South West Africa, and East Africa.

In southern Africa, the British annex Bechuanaland (1885). Gold is found in the Transvaal (1886).

The Heligoland Treaty (1890) defines borders of British and German protectorates in East Africa.

Cecil Rhodes, premier of the British Cape Colony, invades Matabeleland and Mashonaland (1890).

The British defeat the Mahdists at Omdurman (1898); Sudan comes under Anglo-Egyptian rule.

After twenty years of warfare, the French conquest of the western Sudan is completed (1898).

In southern Africa, war breaks out between the British and the Boers (1899).

Striking dockworkers in Sydney clash with armed police (1890).

A severe economic depression causes the failure of many companies and banks (1890-1893).

Trade unions formed by construction workers in Victoria are granted legal recognition (1870).

Victoria introduces free, compulsory education (1872).

The bushranger and bank robber Ned Kelly is captured and hanged (1880).

Proposals for a federal constitution, uniting the six former colonies in the Commonwealth of Australia, are approved by the British parliament (1900).

The crash of financier Jay Cooke's banking company triggers a national economic depression (1873).

Sioux Indians annihilate U.S. troops led by George Custer at Little Bighorn (1876).

Troops quell riots provoked by clashes between striking railway workers and company-paid vigilantes (1877).

Thomas A. Edison invents the incandescent light bulb (1879).

Eight anarchists are condemned to death following strikes and riots in Chicago (1886).

The U.S. Army massacres 200 Indians at Wounded Knee Creek in South Dakota (1890), ending the Indian wars of resistance.

Thousands of unemployed workers march on Washington, D.C., to demand legislative reform (1894).

American support for Cuban revolutionaries leads to war with Spain (1898). Spain cedes Puerto Rico, Guam, and the Philippines to the United States and guarantees the independence of Cuba.

ACKNOWLEDGMENTS

The following materials have been reprinted with the kind permission of the publishers: Page 17: "We are, I fear, . . ." and page 34: "The existing connection . . ." quoted from *The Golden Oriole: Childhood, Family and Friends in India* by Raleigh Trevelyan, London: Secker & Warburg, 1987, and New York: Viking Penguin Inc. Page 28: "We were in the saddle . . .," "Our instructions were to decide . . .," "in spite of all that has happened . . .," and "You ask why I am always thinking . . ." quoted from *The Men Who Ruled India* by Philip Mason, London: Pan, 1978, Philip Mason. Page 29: "Would you like to live in a country . . ." quoted from *The British Conquest and Dominion of India* by Sir Penderel Moon, London: Duckworth, 1989. Page 102: "the inevitable gap between conquest and dominion . . ." quoted from *The River War: The Sudan, 1898* by Winston Churchill, London: Longmans Green, 1902, The Estate of Sir Winston Churchill, by permission of Curtis Brown Ltd.

The editors also wish to thank the following individuals and institutions for their valuable assistance in the preparation of this volume:

England: Brighton—Martin Leighton. Colchester—Jonathan Sergeant. London—James Chambers; Michael Donaghy; Timothy Fraser; Barbara Moir Hicks; Liz Hodgson; Michael Langford, Royal College of Art; Roy Porter, Senior Lecturer in the Social History of Medicine, Wellcome Institute; Deborah Thompson. Tonbridge, Kent—John Norris, The Milne Museum.
United States: Rochester, New York—Todd Gustavson, George Eastman House.

PICTURE CREDITS

The sources for the illustrations that appear in this book are listed below. Credits from left to right are separated by semicolons; from top to bottom they are separated by dashes.

Cover: Detail from painting *The Battle of Isandhlwana* by C.E. Fripp, courtesy of the Director, National Army Museum, London. **2, 3:** Maps by Alan Hollingbery. **8:** Eileen Tweedy /courtesy of the Marchioness of Dufferin and Ava. **10, 11:** Maps by Alan Hollingbery. **12, 13:** Courtesy the Board and Trustees of the Victoria and Albert Museum, London. **14:** British Library, London, Add. 41300 p. 54. **15:** Copyright reserved, reproduced by gracious permission of Her Majesty the Queen. **16:** India Office Library (British Library), London, P480. **18:** The Mansell Collection, London. **19:** Copyright reserved, reproduced by gracious permission of Her Majesty the Queen. **20, 21:** The Mansell Collection, London; India Office Library (British Library), London, Photo 100/ A /2 (9); From *Princely India,* Pennwick Publishing, Inc., New York, 1980—The Mansell Collection, London; From *Princely India,* Pennwick Publishing, Inc., New York, 1980 (2). **22, 23:** Courtesy the Board and Trustees of the Victoria and Albert Museum, London; India Office Library (British Library), London, WD. 2443. **24:** India Office Library (British Library), London, WD. 2479. **25:** W. W. Hooper / The John Hillelson Collection, London. **26:** India Office Library (British Library), London, Photo 15/1 f.646. **27:** India Office Library (British Library), London, Photo 154.p31.d. **28, 29:** Courtesy the Director, National Army Museum, London. **30, 31:** Courtesy the Director, National Army Museum, London—India Office Library (British Library), London, Neg. No. B.3646. **32:** India Office Library (British Library), London, MS. F111/270 EVR. **33:** India Office Library (British Library), London, Neg. No. B5992. **35:** The John Allwood International Exhibition Collection, Kent. **36, 37:** Courtesy Burndy Library, Norwalk, Connecticut; Newcastle upon Tyne City Libraries and Arts; Museum of the City of New York—Consolidated Edison Company of New York Inc. **38, 39:** The Museum of the City of New York; Deutsches Museum, Munich—Michael Freeman / Trustees of the Science Museum, London (4). **40:** Trustees of the Science Museum, London; British Library, London, 12350. M.15. opp. p.57—Milne Electrical Museum, Tonbridge, Kent. **41:** The Institution of Electrical Engineers, London—Trustees of the Science Museum, London. **42:** Archiv für Kunst und Geschichte, West Berlin. **44:** Map by Alan Hollingbery. **45, 46:** Bildarchiv Preussischer Kulturbesitz, West Berlin. **47:** Historisches Archiv, Fried. Krupp GmbH, Essen. **50:** Museo del Risorgimento, Turin. **52:** Courtesy of the Board and Trustees of the Victoria and Albert Museum, London—The Hulton-Deutsch Collection, London. **53, 54:** The Hulton-Deutsch Collection, London. **56-57:** Historisches Archiv, Fried. Krupp GmbH, Essen. **59:** Ullstein Bilderdienst, West Berlin. **60, 61:** Martin Herpich & Sohn OHG (Josef Hartl), Munich Bayerische Verwaltung der Staatlichen Schlosser, Garten und Seen; Rainbird / Robert Harding Picture Library, London; *The Telegraph* Colour Library, London—Martin Herpich & Sohn OHG (Josef Hartl), Munich Bayerische Verwaltung der Staatlichen Schlosser, Garten und Seen. **62:** Bundesarchiv Militärarchiv, Freiburg. **63:** Bildarchiv Preussischer Kulturbesitz, West Berlin. **65:** The Mansell Collection, London. **66, 67:** The Hulton-Deutsch Collection, London. **68, 69:** Brown Brothers, Sterling, Pennsylvania. **70, 71:** Vancouver Public Library, Photo no. 19933. **72, 73:** Eugene J. Hall, Chicago Historical Society. **74:** Royal Pavilion, Art Gallery and Museums, Brighton. **76:** Map by Alan Hollingbery—Eileen Tweedy / Trustees of the Science Museum, London. **78:** Royal Geographical Society, London. **80:** Lauros-Giraudon, Paris. **81:** British Library, London, 2358.D.13. **82:** Bildarchiv Preussischer Kulturbesitz, West Berlin—Brown Brothers, Sterling, Pennsylvania. **83:** Jean-Loup Charmet, Paris. **84:** D. Witty / R. Stanley Collection, Berkshire. **85:** Jean-Loup Charmet, Paris. **86:** Eileen Tweedy / The Rotunda Museum, Woolwich. **87:** Trustees of the British Museum, London, Department of Ethnology (Museum of Mankind). **88, 89:** Marc and Evelyne Bernheim / Woodfin Camp and Associates, Inc., New York; Bildarchiv Preussischer Kulturbesitz, West Berlin. **91:** National Archives, Washington, D.C. **92, 93:** Eileen Tweedy /17th /21st Lancers' Museum, Belvoir Castle, Lincolnshire. **94:** Reproduced by permission of *Punch,* London. **95:** The Hulton-Deutsch Collection, London. **96:** Africana Museum, Johannesburg. **98:** Trustees of the Imperial War Museum, London (3); 1989 Monas Hieroglifica, Milan. **100:** The Hulton-Deutsch Collection, London. **101:** Ullstein Bilderdienst, West Berlin. **103:** The Mansell Collection, London. **104, 105:** Royal Geographical Society, London—from the Kodak Museum at the National Museum of Photography, Film and Television, Bradford; Bequest of W. G. Russell Allen, courtesy Museum of Fine Arts, Boston. **106, 107:** California Museum of Photography, University of California, Riverside; The Bettmann Archive, New York—copyright reserved, reproduced by gracious permission of Her Majesty the Queen—courtesy of the Board and Trustees of the Victoria and Albert Museum, London. **108:** From the Kodak Museum at the National Museum of Photography, Film and Television, Bradford (2)—courtesy George Eastman House; private collection. **109:** Courtesy of the Board and Trustees of the Victoria

and Albert Museum, London (2)—from the Kodak Museum at the National Museum of Photography, Film and Television, Bradford; private collection. **110:** Collection, City of Ballarat Fine Art Gallery, Victoria. **112:** Maps by Alan Hollingbery. **113:** *Major William de Gillern and Niece,* collection, Tasmanian Museum and Art Gallery, Hobart. **114:** Royal Geographical Society, London. **115:** Pitt Rivers Museum, Oxford. **116, 117:** Keast Burke Collection, National Library of Australia, Canberra; Australian Consolidated Press, Sydney. **118, 119:** The Archives Authority of New South Wales, Sydney. **120, 121:** The Mitchell Library, State Library of New South Wales, Sydney; La Trobe Collection, State Library of Victoria, Melbourne. **122:** Brian Brake / John Hillelson Collection, London—*An Incident in the New Zealand Wars,* Major Gustavus Ferdinand von Tempsky, watercolor and pencil on paper, 224 x 290mm., collection, Robert McDougall Art Gallery, Christchurch, New Zealand. **124:** The Dixson Galleries, State Library of New South Wales, Sydney. **125:** Impressions / Ned Kelly's armor in Melbourne Gaol. **126, 127:** La Trobe Collection, State Library of Victoria, Melbourne; *Swanston Street*

from Prince's Bridge, 1861 by Henry Burn, oil on canvas, 71.5 x 91.7cm., presented in 1914 by Mr. John H. Connell, National Gallery of Victoria, Melbourne. **128:** Detail from *A Break Away!* 1891 by Tom Roberts, Art Gallery of South Australia, Adelaide. Elder Bequest Fund, 1899. **130:** Paulus Leeser / The Shearson Lehman Hutton Collection, New York. **132:** Maps by Alan Hollingbery. **133:** Denver Public Library, Western History Department. **134, 135:** Courtesy the Louisiana State Museum; courtesy the New-York Historical Society, New York. **136:** The Museum of the City of New York. **137:** Lloyd Ostendorf, Dayton, Ohio. **138, 139:** Photo by Larry Sherer / painting by Conrad Wise Chapman, courtesy Museum of the Confederacy, Richmond, Virginia. **140:** The Bettmann Archive, New York. **141:** Valentine Museum, Richmond, Virginia. **142, 143:** Photo by Henry Groskinsky / painting by Peter F. Rothermel, Collections of the State Museum of Pennsylvania; Lloyd Ostendorf, Dayton, Ohio. **144, 145:** Library of Congress, Washington, D.C., B8184-144, B8184-B156,

262-8240. **146, 147:** Courtesy Oakland Museum History Department, California; Courtesy Wells Fargo Bank, San Francisco. **148, 149:** Courtesy History Division, Los Angeles County Museum of Natural History; courtesy Museum of the American Indian, Heye Foundation, New York City. **151:** Coffrin's Old West Gallery, Miles City, Montana. **152, 153:** Archives and Manuscripts Division, Oklahoma Historical Society. **154:** Western History Collections, University of Oklahoma Library. **155:** *The Fall of the Cowboy,* 1895 by Frederic Remington, oil on canvas, the Amon Carter Museum, Fort Worth, Texas. **156, 157:** Library of Congress, Washington, D.C., D401-12683. **158, 159:** Keystone-Mast Collection, California Museum of Photography, University of California, Riverside. **161:** The Museum of the City of New York. **163:** Nasjongalleriet, Oslo. **164, 165:** Vincent van Gogh Foundation / National Museum Vincent van Gogh, Amsterdam—Koninklijk Museum voor Schone Kunsten, Antwerp; Albright-Knox Art Gallery, Buffalo, New York. **166, 167:** Bibliothèque Nationale, Paris; Philadelphia Museum of Art, purchased, W. P. Wilstach Collection; Réunion des Musées Nationaux, Paris.

BIBLIOGRAPHY

GENERAL

Anderson, M. S., *The Ascendancy of Europe: 1815-1914.* New York: Longman, 1985.

Bayly, Christopher, ed., *Atlas of the British Empire.* London: Hamlyn Publishing Group / Amazon, 1989.

Briggs, Asa, ed., *The Nineteenth Century.* London: Thames and Hudson, 1970.

Coe, Brian, *The Birth of Photography.* London: Ash & Grant, 1976.

Coe, Brian, and Paul Gates, *The Snapshot Photograph: The Rise of Popular Photography, 1888-1939.* London: Ash & Grant, 1976.

Ford, Colin, ed., *The Story of Popular Photography.* London: Century Hutchinson, 1989.

Fraser, W. Hamish, *The Coming of the Mass Market, 1850-1914.* London: Macmillan, 1981.

Grenville, J. A. S., *Europe Reshaped: 1848-1878.* London: Fontana Harvester Press, 1976.

Headrick, Daniel R., *The Tools of Empire: Technology and European Imperialism in the Nineteenth Century.* New York: Oxford University Press, 1981.

Hennessey, R. A. S., *The Electric Revolution.* London: Oriel Press, 1972.

Hobhouse, Henry, *Forces of Change.* London: Sidgwick & Jackson, 1989.

House, John, and Mary Anne Stevens, eds., *Post-Impressionism: Cross-Currents in European Painting.* London: Royal Academy of Arts / Weidenfeld & Nicolson, 1979.

Huggett, Frank E., *The Land Question and European Society.* London: Thames and Hudson, 1975.

Jeffrey, Ian, *Photography: A Concise History.* New York: Oxford University Press, 1981.

Macdonald, Gus, *Camera: A Victorian Eyewitness.* London: B. T. Batsford, 1979.

Morris, James:
Farewell the Trumpets. London: Penguin, 1979.
Heaven's Command. London: Penguin, 1979.

Pax Britannica. London: Penguin, 1979.

Mosse, W. E., *Liberal Europe: The Age of Bourgeois Realism: 1848-1875.* London: Thames and Hudson, 1974.

Stone, Norman, *Europe Transformed: 1878-1919.* London: Fontana, 1983.

INDIA

Bayly, Christopher, *Rulers, Townsmen and Bazaars: North Indian Society in the Age of British Expansion, 1770-1870.* Cambridge: Cambridge University Press, 1983.

Brown, Judith, *Modern India: The Origins of an Asian Democracy.* London: Oxford University Press, 1985.

Edwardes, Michael, *The Sahibs and the Lotus: The British in India.* London: Constable, 1988.

Hibbert, Christopher, *The Great Mutiny: India, 1857.* London: Penguin, 1980.

Kulke, Hermann, and Rothermund Dietmar, *A History of India.* London: Croom Helm, 1986.

Mason, Philip, *The Men Who Ruled India.* London: Jonathan Cape Pan, 1987.

Moon, Sir Penderel, *The British Conquest and Domination of India.* London: Duckworth, 1989.

Moorhouse, Geoffrey, *India Britannica.* London: Collins Harvill Press, 1983.

Smith, Vincent A., *The Oxford History of India.* Oxford: The Clarendon Press, 1958.

Spear, Percival, *A History of India.* Vol. 2. London: Penguin, 1989.

Trevelyan, Raleigh, *The Golden Oriole: Childhood, Family and Friends in India.* London: Secker & Warburg, 1987.

Watson, Francis, *A Concise History of India.* London: Thames and Hudson, 1974.

Wolpert, Stanley, *A New History of India.* New York: Oxford University Press, 1989.

Worswick, Clark, ed., *Princely India: Photographs by Raja Deen Dayal, 1884-1910.* London: Hamish Hamilton, 1980.

Worswick, Clark, and Ainslie Embree, *The Last Empire: Photography in Brit-*

ish India, 1855-1911. London: Gordon Fraser, 1976.

GERMANY

Blunt, Wilfrid, *The Dream King.* Harmondsworth, England: Penguin, 1973.

Böhme, Helmut, ed., *The Foundation of the German Empire: Select Documents.* Trans. by Agatha Ramm. London: Oxford University Press, 1971.

Craig, Gordon A., *Germany: 1866-1945.* Oxford: Oxford University Press, 1978.

Crankshaw, Edward, *Bismarck.* London: Macmillan, 1981.

Dahrendorf, Ralf, *Society and Democracy in Germany.* London: Weidenfeld and Nicolson, 1968.

Designs for the Dream King: The Castles and Palaces of Ludwig II of Bavaria. London: Debrett's Peerage, 1978.

Glaser, Hermann, *Die Kultur der Wilhelminischen Zeit.* Frankfurt am Main: S. Fischer, 1984.

Horne, Alistair, *The Fall of Paris: The Siege and the Commune, 1870-1871.* London: Macmillan, 1965.

Howard, Michael, *The Franco-Prussian War.* London: Rupert Hart-Davis, 1962.

Kent, George O., *Bismarck and His Times.* Carbondale: Southern Illinois University Press, 1978.

Pflanze, Otto, *Bismarck and the Development of Germany.* Princeton, N.J.: Princeton University Press, 1963.

Rosinski, Herbert, *The German Army.* London: Pall Mall Press, 1966.

Simon, W. M., *Germany in the Age of Bismarck.* London: Allen & Unwin, 1970.

Steinberg, Jonathan, *Yesterday's Deterrent: Tirpitz and the Birth of the German Battle Fleet.* London: Macdonald, 1965.

Stern, Fritz, *Gold and Iron.* New York: Alfred A. Knopf, 1977.

Taylor, A. J. P., *Bismarck: The Man and the Statesman.* London: Hamish Hamilton, 1955.

Wehler, Hans-Ulrich, *The German Empire: 1871-1918.* Trans. by Kim Traynor. Dover, N.H.: Berg Publishers, 1985.

AFRICA

Ajayi, J., and M. Crowder, *History of West Africa.* Harlow, Essex: Longman, 1985.

Chamberlain, M. E., *The Scramble for Africa.* London: Longman, 1974.

Crowder, Michael, *The Story of Nigeria.* London: Faber & Faber, 1962.

Davidson, Basil, *Africa in History.* London: Collins Grafton, 1974.

Flint, John E., ed., *Cambridge History of Africa.* Vol. 5. Cambridge: Cambridge University Press, 1976.

Forbath, Peter, *The River Congo.* London: Secker & Warburg, 1962.

Forstner, Alexander Sydney Kanya, *The Conquest of the Western Sudan.* London: Cambridge University Press, 1969.

Gann, L. H., and Peter Duignan, eds., *Colonialism in Africa.* Vol. 1. Cambridge: Cambridge University Press, 1982.

Hargreaves, John D.:
Prelude to the Partition of West Africa. London: Macmillan, 1966.
West Africa Partitioned. Vols. 1 & 2. Basingstoke: Macmillan, 1974 and 1985.

Hibbert, Christopher, *Africa Explored.* London: Penguin, 1982.

Huxley, Elspeth, *Livingstone and His African Journeys.* London: Weidenfeld and Nicolson, 1974.

Jeal, Tim, *Livingstone.* London: Heinemann, 1973.

Kinross, Lord John, *Between Two Seas: The Creation of the Suez Canal.* London: John Murray, 1968.

Lewis, David Levering, *The Race to Fashoda: European Colonialism and African Resistance in the Scramble for Africa.* London: Bloomsbury, 1988.

Lewis, Roy, and Yvonne Foy, *The British in Africa.* London: Weidenfeld and Nicolson, 1971.

McEvedy, Colin, *The Penguin Atlas of African History.* London: Penguin, 1980.

Monti, Nicolas, ed., *Africa Then: Photographs, 1840-1918.* London: Thames and Hudson, 1987.

Murray, Jocelyn, ed., *Cultural Atlas of Africa.* Oxford: Phaidon, 1981.

Oliver, Roland, and Anthony Atmore, *Africa since 1800.* Cambridge: Cambridge University, 1981.

Oliver, Roland, and Michael Crowder, eds., *The Cambridge Encyclopedia of Africa.* Cambridge: Cambridge University Press, 1981.

Oliver, Roland, and J. D. Fage, *A Short History of Africa.* London: Penguin, 1988.

Oliver, Roland, and G. N. Sanderson, eds., *The Cambridge History of Africa.* Vol. 6. Cambridge: Cambridge University Press, 1985.

Penrose, E. F., ed., *European Imperialism and the Partition of Africa.* London: Frank Cass, 1975.

Robinson, R., and J. Gallagher, *Africa and the Victorians: The Official Mind of Imperialism.* London: Macmillan, 1981.

Rotberg, Robert I., *The Founder: Cecil Rhodes and the Pursuit of Power.* Oxford: Oxford University Press, 1989.

Slade, Ruth M., *King Leopold's Congo.* London: Oxford University Press, 1962.

AUSTRALIA

Broome, Richard, *Aboriginal Australians: Black Response to White Dominance, 1788-1980.* Sydney: Allen & Unwin, 1982.

Burgmann, Verity, and Jenny Lee, eds., *A People's History of Australia since 1788.* Fitzroy, Australia: McPhee Gribble, 1987.

Carroll, John, ed., *Intruders in the Bush: The Australian Quest for Identity.* Melbourne: Oxford University Press, 1982.

Hirst, J. B., *Convict Society and Its Enemies: A History of Early New South Wales.* Sydney: Allen & Unwin, 1982.

Hughes, Robert, *The Fatal Shore: A History of the Transportation of Convicts to Australia, 1787-1868.* London: Collins Harvill, 1987.

Inglis, Kenneth S., *The Australian Colonists: An Exploration of Social History, 1788-1870.* Melbourne: Melbourne University Press, 1974.

Kingston, Beverley, ed., *Oxford History of Australia.* Vol. 3. Melbourne: Oxford University Press, 1988.

Linge, G. J. R., *Industrial Awakening: Geography of Australian Manufacturing, 1788 to 1890.* Sydney: Australian National University Press, 1979.

McQueen, Humphrey, *New Britannia.* Ringwood, Australia: Penguin, 1970.

Moore, David, and Rodney Hall, *Australia: Image of a Nation, 1850-1950.* Sydney: William Collins, 1883.

Shaw, A. G. L., *The Story of Australia.* London: Faber & Faber, 1983.

Ward, Russel, *The Australian Legend.* Melbourne: Oxford University Press, 1978.

White, Richard, *Inventing Australia: Images and Identity, 1788-1980.* Sydney: Allen & Unwin, 1981.

THE UNITED STATES

Billington, R. A., *The Far Western Frontier.* New York: Harper, 1956.

Brock, W. R., *Conflict and Transformation: The United States, 1844-1877.* London: Penguin, 1976.

Brogan, Hugh, *The Pelican History of the United States.* London: Penguin, 1986.

Cruden, Robert, *The Negro in Reconstruction.* Englewood Cliffs, N.J.: Prentice-Hall, 1969.

Davis, Christopher, *North American Indian.* London: Hamlyn Publishing Group, 1969.

Debo, A., *History of the Indians of the United States.* Norman, Okla.: University of Oklahoma Press, 1971.

DeVoto, B., *The Year of Decision: 1846.* London: Eyre & Spottiswoode, 1956.

Dulles, F. R., *America's Rise to World Power.* New York: Harper, 1955.

Franklin, J. H., *The Militant South.* London: Methuen, 1975.

Garraty, John A., and Robert A. McCaughey, *A Short History of the American Nation.* New York: Harper & Row, 1989.

Josephson, M., *The Robber Barons.* London: Eyre & Spottiswoode, 1962.

Kirkland, Edward C., *Industry Comes of Age: Business, Labour, and Public Policy: 1860-1897.* New York: Holt, Rinehart and Winston, 1961.

Macpherson, J. M., *Battle Cry of Freedom.* London: Oxford University Press, 1988.

Mandelbaum, S., *Boss Tweed's New York.* London: John Wiley, 1965.

Miller, D. T., *Frederick Douglass and the Fight for Freedom.* Oxford: Facts on File, 1988.

Perlot, J. N., *Gold Seeker.* New Haven, Conn.: Yale University Press, 1985.

Ransom, Roger L., and Richard Sutch, *One Kind of Freedom: The Economic Consequences of Emancipation.* Cambridge: Cambridge University Press, 1977.

Senkewitz, R. M., *Vigilantes in Gold Rush San Francisco.* Stanford, Calif.: Stanford University Press, 1985.

Waldman, Carl, *Atlas of the North American Indian.* Oxford: Facts on File, 1985.

Wiebe, R. H., *The Search for Order.* London: Macmillan, 1967.

Woodward, Comer Vann, *Origins of the New South: 1877-1913.* Baton Rouge, La.: Lousiana State University Press, 1951.

INDEX

Numerals in italics indicate an illustration of the subject mentioned.

A

Abdelkader (Algerian patriot), *80*
Abolitionists, 139-140
Aborigines, *110,* 113-*114,* *115,* 126
Adelaide, 114
Afghanistan, 9, 17, *30-31*
Africa, *map 76;* agriculture in, 90; colonization of, 84-90; diseases in, 78; education in, *101;* exploration of, 75-*78,* 80-85, *83;* transportation in, *78,* 79-80, 89, 90. *See also individual colonies*
Afridis (Afghan tribe), *31*
Agriculture: advances in, *65,* 66-*67,* *72-73;* in Africa, 90; in Australia, 113-114, 120-123; in Prussia, 45; in Russia, 66; in United States, 66, 132, 134, 137, 145-147, 153, *154*
Ahmad Khan, Sir Sayyid (East Indian Muslim leader), quoted, 30-31
Ahmed Arabi (Egyptian officer), 84
Alabama, 140-141, 145
Alexandria, Egypt, 79
Algeria, 77, 80, 92-93
Allahabad, 24
Alps, 50, 61
Alsace, 86
American River, 131
American Slavery As It Is (Weld), quoted, 138
Andersonville, 107
Anglican church, 83
Anglo-French Declaration of 1899, 92
Angola, 75, 77
Antietam, Battle of, 147
Apache (tribe), 157
Appalachian Mountains, 133
Appomattox, 150
Arapaho (tribe), *148-149*
Architecture: in Australia, 119, *126-127;* in India, *15, 23, 26;* of Louisiana mansion, *134-135*
Argentina, 69, 70, 126
Arkansas, 141
Art, *163-167;* African, *74;* American cowboy, *155;* in Australia, 125; ceramic swan, *60-61;* children's board game, *85;* Nigerian door, *87;* sheep stampede, *128;* tattoos, *104, 122*
Ashanti (African people), 88
Atlanta, 150
Augusta, Marie Luise Katharina (empress of Germany), 49
Aumale, duke of (French governor-general of Algeria), *80*
Australia, *map 112;* agriculture in, 113-114, 120-123; colonization of, 114; Commonwealth of, 112, 129; economics in, 124-127, 129; exploration of, 123, *124;* federation of, 127-129; gold rush in, 114-119, *120,* 165; government in, 116-118; as penal colony, 111-116, *113;* population growth of, 119-123; squatters in, 119-120; transportation in, *116-117,* 121-123; whaling in, *112-113;* wool industry in, 58, 113-114, *116-117,* *118-119,* 120-121, *126-127, 128;* working class in, 125-126

Austria: army of, 47; and Germany, 59; Hapsburg rule of, 43, 47, 51-52; and Hungary, 52; and Italy, 50; and Prussia, 43-45, 48-52; rebellions in, 44
Austro-Hungarian Empire, 163
Auvers-sur-Oise, 164

B

Baden, 53, 55
Bahādur Shāh II (Mogul emperor), *18,* 22, 24-26
Baines, Thomas, study by, *115*
Bala Hissar (Afghan fortress), *30-31*
Ballarat, 115, 117
Banerjea, Surendranath (East Indian patriot), 29; quoted, 34
Barak, William, painting by, *110*
Barnardo, Thomas (British reformer), 107
Baroda, son of gaekwar of, *20-21*
Bavaria, 51, 53, 55
Bechuanaland, 99
Beeton, Isabella (British cooking expert), 72
Belgium, 8, 11, 54, 77, 83, 86-88
Benares, *14*
Bengal, Bay of, 13
Bengal (territory), 13-14, 23, 30-34
Bentinck, Lord William (governor general of India), 17
Berlin, *45,* 58, 86, 165
Berlin, Congress of, 58, 86
Beveridge, Albert (American politician), quoted, 162
Bibighar, *17,* 24
Bismarck, Otto von (German statesman), 9-12, *42,* 43, 44, 53, 55, 86; death of, 64; as German chancellor, 55-63; military campaigns of, 51-52, 54-55; as prime minister, 49-59; quoted, 43, 49, 51, 54, 56, 57, 58, 62-63; rise to power of, 48-49
Blacks, 150-154. *See also* Slavery
Bleichröder, Gerson von (Jewish financier), 58
Blue Mountains (Australia), 113, 114
Boers (Dutch pioneers), 93-101
Boer War, *98-99,* 100-101, 125, 129
Bohemia, 43, 45
Bombay, 13, *23,* 33
Booth, Charles (British sociologist), 165
Booth, John Wilkes (American actor; assassin of Lincoln), 151
Boston, 139, 157
Brady, Mathew (American photographer), 107
Brannan, Sam (American merchant), 131
Brazza, Pierre Savorgnan de (French explorer), *83,* 84-86
Brazzaville, 84
British East India Company, 9-26
British South Africa Company, 97, 99
Broken Hill (Australia), 125
Brooks, Preston S. (American politician), quoted, 139

Brown, John (American abolitionist), 140
Bruce, James (Scottish aristocrat-explorer), 80
Buffalo (animal), 148-149, *151,* 154, 157
Buganda, kingdom of, 83
Bulloch, James (American Confederate naval officer), 143
Bull Run, Battle of, 144
Bundesrat (German federal council), 52-53, 55
Bundi, maharajah of, *20*
Burckhardt, Jakob (Swiss historian), quoted, 55
Burke, Robert O'Hara (Irish adventurer), *124;* quoted, 123
Burma, 10, 17, 18
Burn, Henry, painting by, *127*
Burns, Anthony (American slave), 139
Burton, Richard Francis (British explorer), 80-81
Bushrangers (Australia), 124

C

Cairo, 79, 84, 90
Calcutta, 9, 13, 27
California, 131-133, 137, 139, 146, 160
Cameroons, 86
Campbell, Colin (British field marshal), 24
Canada, 9, 70, 129
Canary Islands, 69
Canning, Lord Charles (governor general of India; first viceroy), 18; quoted, 25-27
Canton, *104*
Carnegie, Andrew (American industrialist), 158
Carpetbaggers, 153
Cavour, Count Camillo di (Italian statesman), 50
Cawnpore, 17, 23-24
Cézanne, Paul, *The Great Bathers, 166-167*
Chamberlain, Joseph (British colonial secretary), 99-100
Chapman, Conrad (American soldier-artist), 138
Charles II (king of Great Britain), 13
Cherokee (tribe), 152
Chicago, 66, 72, 157-158
Child, Sir Josiah (East India Company officer), quoted, 13
China, 9, 83, 104, *106-107,* 115, 119, 160
Christian IX (king of Denmark), 51
Churchill, Winston, quoted, 102
Church of Jesus Christ of Latter-day Saints, 133-134
Cincinnati, 136, 153
Citadel Rock (Wyoming), *146-147*
Civil Service, Indian (ICS), *24,* 27-29
Civil War (U.S.), *map 132, 138-139,* 140, 141; battles in, *142-143,* 144-145, 147-150; causes of, 137-141; and economics, 145; end of, 150; military buildup in, 143-144; naval blockade in, 143-147. *See also individual battles*
Clive, Robert (East India Company officer), 14
Colman, Samuel, painting by, *130*

Colonial empires, *map* 10-11
Columbus, Christopher (Italian navigator), 69
Communards, *54, 55*
Comoro Islands, 89
Confederate States of America, *map* 132, *138-139,* 140, *141,* 141-154
Congo, kingdom of, 83-84, 91, 92-93
Congo Free State, 85-88
Congo River, 80-83, 86-88
Cook, James (English navigator), 112
Cook, Thomas (English entrepreneur), 79
Cooke, Jay (American financier), 158
Cooper's Creek, 121, *124*
Corinna (British steamship), 126
Cornfield with Crows (van Gogh), *164-165*
Cornwallis, Lord Charles (English general and statesman), 14
Coxey, Jacob (American political reformer), 159-160
Crimean War, *107*
Cry, The (Munch), *163*
Crystal Palace (New York), *136*
Cuba, 159, 162
Cumberland River, 147
Curzon, Lord George Nathaniel (viceroy of India), 33-34; quoted, 9, 33, 34
Custer, George Armstrong (American general), 148

D

Daguerre, Louis-Jacques (English inventor), 103
Dahomey, kingdom of, *81*
Dalhousie, Lord (British colonial administrator), quoted, 17-18
Darwin, Charles, *On the Origin of Species,* 165
Davis, Jefferson (president of Confederate states), 150; quoted, 141, 144
Deakin, Alfred (Australian statesman), quoted, 129
Debussy, Claude (French composer), 166
Delagoa Bay, 99
Delhi, 15, 18, 22-26, *32*
Deniehy, Daniel (Australian journalist), 111
Diggers (Australian miners), 116-118, 120
Disraeli, Benjamin (British statesman and author), quoted, 55, 56
Douglas, Stephen (American politician), 140
Douglass, Frederick (American abolitionist), quoted, 151-152
Dreikaiserbund, 59
Durbar, *32*
Durkheim, Émile, *Suicide,* 165

E

Eastman, George (American inventor and industrialist), 108
Edison, Thomas Alva (American inventor), 35, 37, 39
Edward VII (king of Great Britain), 166

Egypt, 79-80, 84-85, 89, 91, *100,* 104
Electricity, *35-41*
Elizabeth I (queen of Great Britain), 12
Ems Telegram, 54
Ensor, James, *Intrigue, 164*
Eritrea, 91
Ethiopia, 77, 80, 90, 91; officers of, *91*
Eureka stockade (Australia), 117-118, *120-121*

F

Faraday, Michael (British scientist), 35
Farmer, Fannie (American cooking expert), 72
Fashions: in Ethiopia, *91;* in India, *20-21;* military, *28, 29;* and photography, *103, 108*
Fenton, Roger, photograph by, *107*
Ferdinand I (emperor of Austria), 45
Flinders, Matthew (English navigator), 113
Flinders River, 123
Florida, 140, 159
Food industry, *65-73*
Forty-niners (American miners), 131-133, *133*
France: in Africa, 77-78, *80, 81,* 83-87, 89-93; colonies of, 9, 11, 127-129; foreign legion of, 80; and Germany, 59; and Great Britain, 13-14; and Italy, 50; and Prussia, 49, 51, 53-54; and Russia, 52; science in, *35, 40, 41;* and United States, 131-133, 140, 161. *See also* Paris
Franco-Prussian War, 50, *52, 53,* 54-55
Franc-tireurs (French resistance fighters), 55
Frankfurt, 58, 165
Frankfurt, Federal Diet of, 44-51
Frankfurt, Treaty of, 55
Frederick II (the Great; king of Prussia), 48
Frederick III (emperor of Germany), 43, 62
Frederick William IV (king of Prussia), 45-49; quoted, 46
Freedmen's Bureau (U.S.), 152-153
French Revolution, 55
Frere, Sir Bartle (British colonial administrator), quoted, 15, 28
Freud, Sigmund, 163-164
Frith, Francis (English photographer), quoted, 104
Fugitive Slave Law, 139

G

Ganges River, 15, 23
Garibaldi, Giuseppe (Italian patriot), 50; quoted, 50
Gaugin, Paul, *The Yellow Christ,* 165
George III (king of Great Britain), 112
Georgia, 140, 150
German Confederation, 44-45, 47, 49-52
Germany, *map* 44; colonies of, 9-12, 59-62, 77, 86, *88-89,* 90, 127; economy

in, 57-58, 64; education in, *59;* empire of, 55-64; government in, 55-58; and Great Britain, 114; industry in, *56-57;* navy in, *62;* science in, *39;* and U.S. Civil War, 143
Geronimo (Apache chief), 157
Gettysburg, Battle of, *142-143,* 150
Ghost Dance religion (American Indian), *148-149*
Gill, S. T., painting by, *124*
Glenrowan, 124, 125
Glidden, Joseph (American inventor), 155
Gogh, Vincent van, *Cornfield with Crows, 164-165*
Gokhale, Gopāl Krishna (East Indian patriot), 31-32, 34
Gordon, Charles (British general), 90
Göttingen, 48
Gough, Hugh (British officer), quoted, 18-19
Government of India Act of 1858, 26
Grant, Ulysses S. (American general; president of United States), 145, 150
Gray, Charles (Australian explorer), 123-124
Great Bathers, The (Cézanne), *166-167*
Great Britain: and Afghan War, *30-31;* African colonies of, 77, 87-90; and Australia, 111, 114-115, 121, 125-126, 129; colonial empire of, 9-12, 127-129; economics in, 143, 165; and Egypt, 79-80, 82, 84-85; and Germany, 57; in India, 12-18, *24, 26, 27, 28, 29;* naval power of, *64,* 77; and New Zealand, *122;* science in, *37;* in South Africa, 93-102; and Sudan, 90-93; and United States, 131-133, 137, 140, 143, 150
Great Salt Lake Basin, 134
Griqua (Afro-European culture), 94
Guam, 159, 162
Gurkhas, 23

H

Hamburg, 58
Hanover, kingdom of, 48, 51, 52, 55
Hargraves, Edward (Australian adventurer), 114-115
Hastings, Warren (East India Company officer), 14
Hawaiian Islands, 160
Heligoland Treaty of 1890, 89-90
Hewitt, W. H. (British general), 18-22
Himalayas, 23, 26
Hinduism, *14, 15,* 17, 18, 24, 30-34
Hispaniola, 69
Hobart, 115
Hodson, William (British officer), 25
Holland. *See* Netherlands
Holmes, Oliver Wendell (American author), quoted, 104
Holstein, duchy of, 51
Homestead Act, 154-155
Homestead Steel Works, *158*
Hume, Allan Octavian (East India Company officer), 30
Hungary, 43, 45, 47, 52, 59
Huntington, Collis P. (American railroad magnate), quoted, 160
Hyderabad, nizam of, *21*

I

Illinois, 140
India, *map* 10; British conquest of, 12-18; British rule of, 26-34; economics in, 27-28; education in, 29, 33-34; famines in, *25,* 28, 32-33; government in, 14, 28-29; industry in, 27-28, 33-34; military uniforms in, *28, 29;* political movements in, 30-33; royalty in, *12-13, 20-21, 26-27, 32;* servants in, *8, 19,* 27; social life in, 17, *21,* 28-29; thuggee in, *14,* 17; tiger hunts in, *21;* transportation in, *22-23,* 27-28, 33
India Act, 14
Indian Mutiny of 1857, 10, 15, 16, 18-26
Indian National Congress, 30-34
Indian Ocean, 93
Industry: cattle, *68-69;* electricity in, *40-41;* fish, *70-71;* in Germany, 56-57, 58, 59, 64; in India, 27-28, 33-34; in Prussia, 44; in United States, 132, *136,* 137, *140,* 143-145, *158,* 159-160; wool, 113-114, *116-117, 118-119, 120-121, 126-127, 128*
Intrigue (Ensor), *164*

Iowa, 137
Isabella II (queen of Spain), 53
Islam: in Africa, 75-80, 84-85, 88, 90, 92-93; in India, 18-26, 30-34
Iswandhlwana, battle of, 95-96
Italy, 9, 11, 43, 47, 59, 77, 91

J

Jameson, Leander Starr (Scottish physician and administrator), 99
Jammu and Kashmir, maharajah of, *20*
Janszoon, Willem (Dutch navigator), 111
Japan, 104
Jews, 58, 163
Johannesburg, 99
Johnson, Andrew (president of United States), quoted, 152-153
Junkers (Prussian nobles), 45, 48, 58

K

Kabul, 31
Kagera River, 81
Kalahari Desert, 81
Kālī (Hindu goddess), 14, 17
Kanpur. *See* Cawnpore
Kansas, 137, 139, 154
Kansas City, stockyards in, *68-69*
Kansas-Nebraska Bill of 1854, 139
Kavanagh (civilian clerk), 24
Kelly, Ned (Australian bushranger), 124; armor of, *125*
Kentucky, 144
Kenya, 78-79, 89-90
Khartoum, 90
Khedive Ismail (pasha of Egypt), quoted, 79
Khoikhoi (African people), 94
Kilimanjaro, Mount, 79
Kilburn, Benjamin West, photograph by,

Kimberley, 97, 98, 100
King, John (Australian explorer), 123, 124
Kiowa (tribe), 155
Kipling, Rudyard (British author), quoted, 13, 21
Kitchener, Horatio Herbert (British field marshal), 90-93
Kodok, 91-92
Krapf, Johann Ludwig (German missionary), 79
Kraus, Karl (Austrian writer), quoted, 163
Kruger, Paul (South African statesman), 95-100; quoted, 100
Krupp family, 56, 58
Ku Klux Klan, 154
Kulturkampf, 57

L

Ladysmith, 98, 100
Lambing Flat, 119
Land rushes, *152-153*
Landwehr (Prussian militia), 48
Lawrence, Sir Thomas (British painter), 103
Lee, Robert E. (American Confederate general), *145*, 147, 150
Leichardt, Ludwig (German explorer), 123
Leopold (German prince), 53
Leopold II (king of Belgium), 83, 85; quoted, 86-88
Lesseps, Ferdinand de (French diplomat), 79, 82
Liberia, 77
Lincoln, Abraham (president of United States), *137*, 140, 144-145, 147-150, 151; quoted, 137, 140, 143, 147
Little Bighorn, battle of, 148
Livingstone, David (Scottish missionary and explorer), 75-77, *78*, 81, 101; quoted, 78
Livingstone Falls, 82-84
Lobengula (king of the Matabele), 97-99; quoted, 97
Lohengrin (Wagner), 60
London, 21, 29, 125-126, 165
London College of Surgeons, 91
London Journal, quoted, 75
Lorraine, 86
Louisiana, *134-135*, 137, 140
Louis-Philippe (king of France), 45
Lualaba River, 81-82, 83
Lucknow, 23-24
Ludwig II (king of Bavaria), 55, *60*, 61
Luxor, 79

M

McClellan, George B. (American general), 147
McCormick, Cyrus (American inventor), 65
Madagascar, 89
Madras, 13, 25

Mafeking, 98, 100
Mahdi. *See* Muhammad Ahmed ibn as-Seyyid Abd Allāh
Mahler, Gustav (Austrian composer), 166
Main River, 52
Majuba Hill, battle of, 95
Malay Archipeligo, 12
Mallarmé, Stéphane (French poet), 166
Manassas, Battle of, 144
Maori (New Zealand people), *122;* carving, *122*
Marathas (Hindu rulers), 13, 15, 31-32
Marchand, Jean-Baptiste (French officer), 91-92
Martin, Paul, photograph by, *109*
Marx, Karl, 165
Maryland, 137, 144
Mashonaland, 97-99
Massachusetts, 137
Matabele (African people), 97-99
Maxim, Hiram (American inventor), 86
Maxim machine gun, *86,* 91, 99
Medicine: in Africa, 76, 78; chest, *76*
Medicine Bow River, *130*
Mediterranean, 82, 93
Meerut, 18-22
Melbourne, 113, 115-117, 121, 123, 125-126, *126-127*
Menelik (emperor of Ethiopia), 90
Metternich, Klemens (Austrian statesman), 44-45
Metz, 54
Mexican War, 141, 147
Mexico, 131-133, 148-149
Milner, Alfred (British administrator), 99-100; quoted, 100
Mining: in Australia, 114-119, *120,* 125; in Prussia, 44, 47; in South Africa, 94-97, *95;* in United States, 131, *133*
Missionaries: in Africa, *74,* 75-77, 79, 80-83, *101;* in India, 15, 27
Mississippi, 140, 148-149, 150
Mississippi River, 143, 147
Missouri, 137, 144
Mitrailleuse (French machine gun), 54
Mogul empire, 13-14, 18, 22
Moltke, Helmuth von (Prussian field marshal), *46,* 51, 53, 54; quoted, 47
Monet, Claude (French painter), 166
Montana, 148-149
Mormon church. *See* Church of Jesus Christ of Latter-day Saints
Mornington, Lord Richard (governor general of India), 14-15
Morocco, 79
Morse, Samuel (American inventor), 136
Mozambique, 75-78
Muhammad Ahmed ibn as-Seyyid Abd Allāh (the Mahdi), 84, 90-91
Muhammad Ali (pasha of Egypt), 79
Munch, Edvard, *The Cry,* *163*
Muslim League (India), 30-31
Muslims. *See* Islam
Muybridge, Eadweard (English photographer), 103
Myall Creek, 114

N

Nachtigal, Gustav (German explorer), 86
Napoleon, 14, 45, 48, *54*

Napoleon III (Louis-Napoleon, nephew of Napoleon), 45, 54-55, 103; quoted, 55
Napoleonic Wars, 44
Natal, 95
Nationalism: in Egypt, 84-85; in Germany, 57, 61; in India, 33-34; in Italy, 50; in Prussia, 44-*45,* 49-50
Native Americans, 133, *148-149,* 151, 155-157. *See also individual tribes*
Natives Land Act of 1913, 100-101
Nebraska, 139, 146, 154
Neill, James (British general), 17
Netherlands, 11, 83, 111-112
Neuschwanstein Castle, *60,* *61*
New Caledonia, 127
New Guinea, 127
New Holland. *See* Australia
New Jersey, 137
New Mexico, 133
New Orleans, 147, 153
New South Wales, 112-115, 118-127, 129
New York, *37, 38-39, 107,* 134-136, 153, *156-157, 161*
New York Herald, 81
New Zealand, 122
Niagara Falls, *104-105*
Nicholas I, Czar, 46
Nielson, H., photograph by, *104-105*
Nietzsche, Friedrich (German philosopher), quoted, 163
Nigeria, 87
Niger River, 80, 89, 91-93
Nile River, 79, 80-83, 89
Nordau, Max (Jewish author), 163
North Carolina, 141
Northern Virginia, Army of, 147
North German Confederation, 52-53
North Island (New Zealand), 122
Nyangwe, 83
Nyasa, 81
Nyasa Lake, 81

O

Odilon, lithograph by, *166*
Oklahoma Territory, *152-153*
Olmütz, Treaty of, 47
Oman, 78
Omdurman, battle of, 91, *92-93,* 102
Orange Free State, 94
Orange River, 94
Oregon, 66, 131-133
Origin of Species, On the (Darwin), quoted, 165
Ottoman Empire, 58-59, 79
Oudh, kingdom of, 15-17
Oyster Bay (Australia), 115

P

Pacific Railroad Act of 1862, 154
Panama, 162
Paraguay, 69
Paris, 48, *52,* 53, *54,* 55
Parsees, 30
Pennsylvania, 137, 143, 150, 158

Perth, 112
Peters, Carl (German physician-entrepreneur), 86, 89
Philadelphia, 162
Philippine Islands, 159, 162
Phillip, Arthur (governor of Australia), 113, 114
Photography, *103-109*
Piedmont-Sardinia, kingdom of, 50
Pittsburgh, 158
Pitt, William (English statesman), 14
Pius IX, Pope, quoted, 57
Plague, 32-33
Plassey, Battle of, 14, 22
Poland, 44
Pomerania, 52
Pont Aven, 165
Populism, 159
Port Phillip, 113
Portugal, 9, 11, 75-78, 85-86
Potomac, Army of the, 147
Prague, Treaty of, 52
Pretoria, 97, 100
Promontory Point (Utah), 154
Prussia: army of, 47-48; and Austria, 51-55; economy in, 45, 47; and France, *52;* government in, 45-48, 52-53; industry in, 44; rebellions in, 45; science in, 48. *See also* Germany
Puerto Rico, 159, 162
Punjab (province), 17, 23, 24, 27

Q

Queensland, 114, 121-123, 125-126

R

Railroads: in Africa, 79-80, 90; in Australia, 121-123; in Germany, 56; in India, *22-23,* 27-28, 33; in Prussia, 47; in South Africa, 99; in United States, 136, 143, *146-147,* 150, 154, 158-160
Ramsay, James. *See* Dalhousie, Lord
Rebman, Johannes (German missionary), 79
Red Cloud (Sioux chief), quoted, 155
Red Fort (Delhi), 22
Red Sea, 79, 82, 91
Regulating Act of 1773, 14
Reichstag (German popular assembly), 52-55, 56-58, 62, 64
Remington, Frederic, painting by, *155*
Renoir, Auguste (French painter), 166
Republic Gold Mining Company, 94
Rhineland, 44
Rhine River, 44
Rhodes, Cecil John (British administrator and financier), *94,* 95-100; quoted, 96, 97
Richmond 144
Riis, Jacob, photograph by, *107*
Rimbaud, Arthur (French poet), 165
Ripon, Lord George F. S. Robinson (viceroy of India), 29-30; quoted, 29
Risorgimento, 50
Roberts, Tom, painting by, *128*
Robida, Albert, drawing by, *40*
Rocky Mountains, 131, 148-149
Roe, Sir Thomas (East India Company

officer), quoted, 12-13
Roman Catholic Church, 53, 56-57, 74, 83
Rorke's Drift, battle of, 95, *96*
Rothermel, Peter Frederick, painting by, *142-143*
Rousseau, Henri, *War, 167*
Roy, Ram Mohun (Hindu reformer), 17
Royal Geographical Society, 79, 80, 81
Royal Navy (Great Britain), 112
Royal Niger Company, 89
Rudd, Charles (English financier), 97
Russia, 9, 17, 31; agriculture in, 58, 66; army of, 45-46; and Australia, 129; and France, 52; and Germany, 57

S

Sacramento, 131, 154
Sadova, battle of, 51
Sahara (desert), 90
San Francisco, 131, 154, 158
Satanta (Kiowa chief), quoted, 155-157
Saxony, 51, 52
Sayyid Said (sultan of Oman), 78
Scalawags (Southern reconstructionists), 153
Schleswig, duchy of, 51
Science: and electricity, *35-41*, 64; and food production, 65; in Prussia, 48; and telegraph, 136
Scobie, James (Australian miner), 117
Scott, Dred (American slave), 140
Scott, Winfield (American general), 143
Sedan, 54-55
Sepoys (Indian soldiers), 16-26
Seven Weeks' War, 51-52
Sharpsburg, Battle of, 147
Shaw, George Bernard, 166
Sherman, William (American general), 150
Shiloh, Battle of, 147
Sicily, 50
Siemens, Ernst Werner von (German scientist), 35
Sierra Leone, 77
Sikhs, 23, 25
Silesia, 44
Simla, 23, 26
Sind (territory), 17, 27
Sioux (tribe), 148, 155
Slavery: in Africa, 77-79, 101; in Australia, 126; in United States, 133, *135*, 137-141, 144-145, 150-151
Smith, Joseph (founder of Mormon Church), 133
Socialism, *54*, 57, 58, 62, 165
Sontag, Louis, painting by, *38-39*
South Africa, 77, 93-102, *95*
South America, 69
South Carolina, 137-138, 140-141
South Dakota, 149
Spain, 9, 11, *53*, 131-133, 159, 162
Spanish-American War, 147, *159*, 162

Speke, John Hanning (British explorer), 80-81; quoted, 80
Stanley, Henry Morton (British explorer and journalist), 81-84; quoted, 81, 83
Stanley Falls, 82-84
Statue of Liberty, *161*
Stephens, Alexander (vice president of Confederate states), quoted, 141
Stevenson, Robert Louis (Scottish author), quoted, 9
Stowe, Harriet Beecher, *Uncle Tom's Cabin,* 137-138
Sturt, Charles (English explorer), 123
Sudan, 84-85, 88, 90-93, 125
Suez Canal, 27-28, 79, *82*, 84
Suicide (Durkheim), 165
Sumner, Charles (American politician), quoted, 139
Sumter, Fort, *138-139*, 141-143, 144
Surat, 12
Swahili (Afro-Arab culture), 78, *88-89*, 101
Swan, Joseph (English inventor), 39
Sydney, 112, 113, 126

T

Talbot, W. H. Fox (French painter and inventor), 103
Tall al-Kebir, 84
Tanganyika, Lake, 80-83
Tanganyika (territory), 88, 89-90, 101
Tanjore, rajah of, *12-13*
Tanzania, 78, 86
Tasmania, *112*, 113-114, 115
Technology: and food production, 65, *66-67, 70-71, 72-73*; and photography, *103*; steam hammer, *56-57*; steam pumps, 97; steamships, 134; in United States, *136*
Tennessee, 141, 150
Tennessee River, 147
Tesla, Nikola (American inventor), 36
Texas, 133, 140, 157
Thiers, Louis-Adolphe (French statesman and historian), 55
Thompson, John, photograph by, *164*
Tilak, Bal Gangadhar (East Indian patriot), 31-33
Tipu Sultan (sultan of Mysore), 14-15
Togo, 86, 89
Tourism, in Africa, 79, *100*
Trade: in Africa, 75-79, 86-90; in Egypt, 79-80; in Germany, 58; in India, 16, 29; of opium, 16; in Prussia, 45; in United States, 162
Trade unions, 125-126, 129, 158-162, 165

Transportation: in litter, *89*; by oxcart, *116-117*; by oxen, *78*; railroads, *22-23*, 27-28, 33, 47, 79-80, 90, 99, 121-123, 136, 143, *146-147*, 150, 154, 158-160; in the United States, *37-38*, 41; wagon trains, *130*
Transvaal, 93-101
Trevelyan, Charles (English politician and historian), 17-18; quoted, 34
Trollope, Anthony (English novelist), quoted, 125
Tunisia, 79
Tuscany, 50
Twain, Mark, quoted, 94
Tweed, William "Boss" (American politician), 157

U

Udaipur, maharajah of, *20*
Uganda, 83, 89-90
Umar al-Hajj (Muslim reformer), 79
Uncle Tom's Cabin (Stowe), 137-138
Unions. *See* Trade Unions
Union of South Africa, 100-101
United States, *map 132*; agriculture in, 58, 66, 132-134, 137, 145-147, 153, *154*; Civil War in, 107, 133, 141-154; colonies of, 9, *159*, 162; Constitution, 140; economics in, 137-139, 145, 146, 154, 157-162; education in, 137, 160; gold rush in, 131, *133*, 165; government in, 136-140, 152-153, 157-159; immigrants in, 154-157, *156-157*, 161; industry in, 132, *136*, 137, *140*, 143, 145, *158*, 159-160; pioneers in, *130*, 133-137, *152-153, 154-157*; reconstruction in, 151-154; science in, 35-36, 37, *38-39*; Supreme Court, 140; transportation in, *38-39, 41, 130, 146-147*
Utah, 154

V

Vaal River, 94
van Gogh, Vincent, *Cornfield with Crows, 164-165*
Varzin, 53-54
Versailles, 43, *53*, 55
Vicksburg Campaign, 150
Victor Emmanuel II (king of Italy), 50
Victoria, Lake, 80-83, 89-90
Victoria (Australia), 111, 114-121, 124-125
Victoria (queen of Great Britain), 19, 32, 62, 91, 129, 166; quoted, 75
Victoria Falls, 75
Vienna, 45, 58, 163
Vienna, Congress of, 44
Vienna, Treaty of, 51
Virginia, 140, 141, 144-145

W

Wagner, Richard, *Lohengrin,* 60-61
Waitangi, Treaty of, 122
Warfare: Americans in, *159*; Boers in, *98-99*; British in, 28, 29, 96; dervishes in, *92-93*; Ethiopians, *91*; German battle cruiser in, *62*; machine guns in, 54, *86*, 91, 99; Prussians in, *47*, 48, 51, 54-55; railroads in, 47, 143; Swahili in, *88-89*; Zulu in, 96
War (Rousseau), *167*
Washington, D.C., 147, 151, 160
Weld, Theodore, *American Slavery As It Is,* 137-138
Wellesley, Marquis Richard (governor general of India), 14-15
Wellington, duke of, 15
Wells Fargo Company, strongbox of, *147*
Wilberforce, William (British statesman and evangelist), quoted, 16-17
Wilde, Oscar, 166
William I (king of Prussia; German emperor), 43, *46*, 48-49, 51-57, 62; quoted, 55, 56
William II (emperor of Germany), 62-64, *63*, 99, 101; drawing by, *62*
Williamstown (Australia), 121
Wills, William John (English surveyor), 123, *124*
Witwatersrand, 95, 97
Women: Aborigine, 115; in Australia, 129; in England, *109*; in Germany, 59; in India, 17, 18, 24-25, 27, 28, 32
Wounded Knee Creek, 149
Württemberg, 53, 55
Wyoming Territory, 131, *146*

Y

Yellow Christ, The (Gauguin), *165*
Yoruba (African people), 87; carvings by, *74*, *87*
Young, Brigham (Mormon leader), 134

Z

Zambezi River, 75, 78, 80, 81, 97
Zambia, 81
Zanzibar, 78, 80-81
Zola, Émile (French novelist), 165
Zollverein (Prussian commercial union), 45, 47, 49
Zulu (African people), 95, 96
Zweig, Stefan (Austrian writer), quoted, 163